# CONTENTS

## Photo credits

Dr. G. Allen 36 (top), 37 (top), 146, 154; Louise Van der Meid 51, 70, 75, 91, 108, 115, 117, 122, 125, 127, 150, front endpapers; courtesy of Vogelpark. Walsrode 19 (top), 27, 33, 36 (bottom), 37 (bottom), 41, 44, 48, 65, 68 (bottom), 73, 76 (bottom), 77, 80, 81, 84, 85, 88, 89, 92, 93, 96; Harry V. Lacey 14, 28, 26, 45, 49, 52, 53, 56, 67, 60, 61, 68 (top), 69, 72, 76 (top), 109, 147; Dr. Herbert Axelrod back endpapers, 4, 130, 139; D.R. Baylis 151; R. Hanson 5, 142, 143; Dr. M. Vriends 10, 131; J. Chelman and D. Petrulla 11, 135, 138, 155; San Diego Zoo 15; Paul Kwast 19 (bottom); John Daniel 134.

ISBN 0-87666-963-1

Distributed in the U.S. by T.F.H. Publications, Inc., 211 West Sylvania Avenue, PO Box 427, Neptune, NJ 07753; in England by T.F.H. (Gt. Britain) Ltd., 13 Nutley Lane, Reigate, Surrey; in Canada to the pet trade by Rolf C. Hagen Ltd., 3225 Sartelon Street, Montreal 382, Quebec; in Canada to the book trade by H & L Pet Supplies, Inc., 27 Kingston Crescent, Kitchener, Ontario N28 2T6; in Southeast Asia by Y.W. Ong, 9 Lorong 36 Geylang, Singapore 14; in Australia and the South Pacific by Pet Imports Pty. Ltd., P.O. Box 149, Brookvale 2100, N.S.W. Australia; in South Africa by Valid Agencies, P.O. Box 51901, Randburg 2125 South Africa. Published by T.F.H. Publications, Inc., Ltd., the British Crown Colony of Hong Kong.

# building an aviary

dr. carl naether

*Second edition, revised and expanded*
*by dr. matthew m. vriends*

This indoor aviary would be suitable for keeping several small birds or a couple larger birds, such as parrots.

**Opposite:**
These parrots, a macaw (top), a cockatoo (middle) and a slender-billed cockatoo (bottom), are comfortable together in a large outdoor aviary.

# I

## *Aviaries Provide the Most "Natural" Enclosures for Captive Birds*

The purpose of this initial chapter is to explain how and why birds can be kept in aviaries in good health for many years. An aviary, let us be clear on this point, is simply a reasonably large enclosure usually placed outdoors, often called a birdhouse, with one or more sides (walls) made of wire or glass or other more or less "open" or transparent material. Its purpose is to house a number of birds satisfactorily the year round. In many cases, the modern aviary consists of two adjoining parts, namely a wired-in or glassed-in flight and a roofed-over permanent shelter or house attached to it.

The flight must be considerably *larger* than the shelter, because it is in this section that the birds will take their exercise. How the space is divided between flight and aviary will depend upon a number of factors. In the first place, from the birds' point of view, the longer the flight the better, and if the aviary is a comparatively small one, at least four-fifths of the total length should be given up to the flight. But here a difficulty is created for the owner because it leaves him with a shelter which is very small, and from his point of view, attending to the birds will always be difficult unless he has sufficient elbow-room. In small aviaries of this type it is usual to gain access to the shelter by standing in the flight itself, for there is rarely room to make an outside door convenient.

Thus, probably the first thing to do is to decide on the

length of the flight that is necessary for the birds to keep them in sound condition, and then after that to consider the type and size of the shelter, each of which points will be governed by the available space and the cost. Many fanciers like their shelter in the form of a bird-room so that when the inmates have been driven in from the flight they, the owners, can sit down and watch their pets in the inside cages or small flights. If a shelter of this sort is within the means of the bird-keeper, it is certainly the one which will give him the greatest pleasure in his hobby.

However, there are also so-called indoor aviaries, usually large, stationary or portable cages, often reaching from floor to ceiling, in which birds are kept for pleasure and sometimes for breeding and profit. Such aviaries are a great boon to persons who, for one reason or another, do not have suitable places for their birds outdoors or who simply prefer to have their feathered pets right with them in the house, where they can watch and enjoy their various doings at close range at any time and can also better cater to their daily needs.

Housing birds in an aviary offers many practical advantages over housing them in cages. Of course, if you keep but very few birds, one or more cages may serve to keep them in healthy condition, and you can always move a cage from one place to another without much trouble. But if you keep half a dozen or more birds—most birdlovers get into the habit of adding more and more to their collections—the aviary is the most suitable enclosure for them.

Almost any kind of bird lives longer in captivity if he has an opportunity to exercise his wings whenever he feels the urge to do so. Most cages do not afford him that needful opportunity, giving him usually only hopping, but no flying, exercise. The result is that the caged bird, getting all he wants to eat, soon grows fat and dull—and often shortlived. On the other hand, a bird kept in a more or less spacious aviary has to exercise his wings—has to fly various distances hundreds of times every day to reach this or that part of the

This sturdy aviary built for budgerigars provides all the essential requirements for these birds to feel at home, though confined.

These aviaries were designed to be used for breeding grass parakeets.

aviary, and especially to get to the places where food and drink are made available. Such frequent flying is bound to keep his wing and other muscles firm and flexible, to stimulate his appetite, and to prevent him from gaining too much weight. In short, it keeps him in satisfactory physical condition.

Then, the bird enthusiast should consider the amount of work involved in keeping his birds. There is no gainsaying the fact that to care for a collection—small or large—of birds in an aviary requires a good deal less work than keeping them in individual cages, for in an aviary a number of birds can use the same feeding and drinking facilities, which in most cages are separate for each occupant. Furthermore, consider the matter of cleaning. Whereas a cage has to be cleaned frequently, at least once a week or oftener, to keep its occupant or occupants healthy and trim, an aviary, depending of course on its size and the number of birds kept in it, requires cleaning much less often. Usually there is also much less labor required in feeding and watering birds kept in aviaries for the simple reason that they may be supplied with sufficient feed and water to last them several days, which is especially true of the seedeaters. Birds so kept, moreover, may be safely left to their own devices for a number of days in case their owner wishes to go away for a few days. Many a single man and woman whose job necessitates leaving feathered pets at home all day or several days finds the aviary the most practical means of housing birds. Kept in an aviary of suitable size, the birds are assured of getting sufficient feed and water, as well as plenty of wing exercise and the company of other birds.

Of course, the outstanding reason why most lovers of birds prefer to house them in aviaries is that they wish to give them an opportunity to build nests and raise broods of youngsters—strong, healthy youngsters. Such persons are simply not satisfied with just keeping birds to look at or to listen to—they want to give them an opportunity to follow their natural inclinations, namely to reproduce their kind. And for this purpose there is no better place in which to raise birds in captivity than an aviary of the right sort.

Aviaries enable men and women to raise birds for pleasure as well as for profit—as few or as many birds as they wish or can afford to raise. If room is available, more and more bird pens or compartments can be added. Some people are satisfied with one aviary in which they keep a group of finches, parakeets, softbills, or doves, or else a mixed collection consisting of some of each of these different kinds. Ordinarily, however, it is not a good policy to mix parrot-like (hookbilled) birds with finches and softbills, especially in a small aviary. Other people, being keenly interested in seeing their birds breed successfully, prefer to house them in a group or series of aviaries, usually consisting of a number of wired-in flights with suitable permanent shelters or houses attached.

Whether you decide to keep your birds in one aviary or a number of aviaries, the important consideration is to build an enclosure which will, first of all, suit the birds you plan to place in it, and, secondly, suit you, in so far as you have the space, the time, and the money available for this particular and very fascinating pastime.

Small birds like the finches, waxbills and mannikins shown above should never be housed with parrots and parrot-like birds like grand eclectus parrots (facing page); under such circumstances, it would not be unusual for smaller birds to be injured by their larger cousins.

14

# II

# *Aviaries Suited to Various Types of Birds and Climatic Conditions*

In America today we keep in captivity a wide variety of foreign birds. All of them will thrive in aviaries if these enclosures are built with the birds' welfare the principal objective.

Among the so-called seedeaters or hardbills, canaries and finches are the favorites with most people because they are usually quite hardy, require rather simple care, and are comparatively easy to breed and to raise to maturity. Next in popular favor rank the so-called hookbills, including parrakeets (also called budgerigars), lovebirds, cockatiels, and the larger parrots, cockatoos, and macaws. In view of the fact that all parrot-like birds have dispositions and habits quite distinct from those of finches and canaries, they are best kept by themselves.

Keeping canaries or finches with parrot-like birds in a small aviary often results in injuries to the former, for it happens not infrequently that a hookbill will bite the toes or the legs of a canary or finch that approaches too closely. In a large aviary, where the birds aren't all crowded together and thus are able to get readily out of one another's way, the parrot-like birds are not so likely to harm canaries, finches, and other similar birds. But for safety's sake and for most satisfactory results in keeping and breeding your birds, it is very desirable to separate the parrot-like birds from ordinary seedeaters as well as from softbills. Moreover, owing to their striking individual appearance, peculiar ways of flying and of acting in general, parrot-like birds show to much better advantage if kept in an aviary or aviaries by themselves. After all, they are no close relation to the common seedeaters, the finches and canaries, with whom they are usually not at all eager to associate in a friendly way.

Canaries, finches, siskins, and the like may usually be kept together in the same aviary, provided it affords them plenty of room for flying, mating, and breeding activities. These types of hardbills require just about the same kinds of feed and general care. However, it is unwise to make general predictions regarding the behavior in an aviary of any mixed group of seedeaters for the simple reason that each and every variety of finch, etc., has its own peculiar habits which no birdkeeper can tell in advance with any degree of certainty. It is assuredly true that while, commonly speaking, canaries, finches, siskins, and other hardbills of approximately the same size, general appearance, and habits get along well together in an aviary under ordinary conditions, at breeding time, that is, in spring and in summer, each mated pair of birds begins to assert its so-called territorial rights in the aviary so vigorously that if the birds belonging to a mixed collection are too crowded, lacking a sufficient number of nesting and roosting places, they will begin to fight one another and continue to do so for days on end, not infrequently with resultant permanent injuries.

In other words, it is perfectly all right for you to keep a mixed and fairly large group of seedeaters in one and the same aviary, provided you do not attempt to breed them. In such a case, the males of various species such as canaries, finches, siskins, buntings, and other kinds would probably serve your purposes best. Their varied and often very colorful plumage delights the eye and their song delights the ear. The moment, however, that you begin to introduce females into your collection, trouble starts, since at breeding time the males will vie for nesting (territorial) rights and sites, and

also for the "possession" of females.

That, by the way, is the reason why aviculturists bent on breeding their birds rarely keep mixed collections, unless temporarily for lack of space or other good reasons. After years of costly experience, they have learned that it pays to respect the individual characteristics and habits of each separate variety of bird  by keeping it in an aviary  or pen  or compartment *by itself*. Such separation has the added advantage of giving the fancier a good opportunity to study the various feeding, breeding, and other requirements of each avian variety.

However, there are exceptions to all rules, and some pairs of birds, even though of different species, will nevertheless breed successfully together in the same aviary provided it is large enough so that each pair can "take over" plenty of room for its own uses.

It is difficult for us to name birds here which might fit into a mixed collection or group, since no one can foretell the behavior of birds under conditions of which he knows nothing. We only give a couple of collections, based on personal experience. It may well be that the named birds in some other aviaries fight constantly. Only experience will tell!

One type of bird collection
could include canaries
(facing page), cordon bleus
(right) and aurora waxbills
(below).

# SOME COLLECTIONS OF BIRDS

I

Fire Finch *(Lagonostica senegala);* Avadavat *(Amandava aman-dava);* Cordon Bleu *(Uraeginthus bengalus);* Star Finch *(Bathilda ruficauda);* Lavender Finch *(Estrilda caerulescens);* Grey Waxbill *(Estrilda troglodytes);* Orange-cheeked Waxbill *(Estrilda melpoda);* Zebra Finch *(Taeniopygia guttata castanotis);* Bengal Finch *(Lonchura domestica);* Nutmeg Mannikin or Spice Finch *(Lonchura punctulata);* Tricolored Mannikin *(Lonchura malacca malacca);* Black-headed Mannikin *(Lonchura m. atricapilla);* White-headed Mannikin *(Lonchura maja);* Grey-headed Silverbill *(Odontospiza caniceps);* African Silverbill *(Euodice malabarica cantans);* Indian Silverbill *(Euodice malabarica);* Chinese Painted Quail *(Coturnix chinensis)*

II

Star Finch *(Bathilda ruficauda);* Violet-eared Waxbill *(Uraeginthus granaticus);* Blue-headed Waxbill *(Uraeginthus cyanocephalus);* Cordon Bleu *(Uraeginthus bengalus);* Melba Finch *(Pytilia melba);* Aurora Waxbill *(Pythilia phoenicoptera);* Peter's Twin-spot *(Hypargos niveoguttatus);* Lavender Finch *(Estrilda caerulescens);* Gray Singing Finch *(Serinus leucopygia);* Canary *(Serinus canaria domesticus);* Peking Nightingale *(Leiothrix lutea);* Chinese Painted Quaiil *(Coturnix chinensis)*

III

Australian Grassfinches; Parrot Finches; Bengal Finch *(Lonchura domestica);* Gray Singing Finch *(Serinus leucopygia);* Diamond Dove *(Geopelia cuneata);* Chinese Painted Quail *(Coturnix chinensis)*

IV

Large Weavers; Zebra Finch *(Taeniopygia guttata castanotis);* Bengal Finch *(Lonchura domestica);* Cockatiel *(Nymphicus hollandicus);* Budgerigar *(Melopsittacus undulatus);* Californian Quail *(Lophortyx californica);*

V

Weavers; Whydahs, Cardinals; Cutthroat Finch *(Amadina fasciata);* Java Sparrow *(Padda oryzovora);* Californian Quail *(Lophortyx californica);* Small Doves

In all cases in which mixed collections of birds have done reasonably well, the birds were given ample room for flying, nesting, and roosting activities with the result that fighting was kept to a minimum. For example, a fancier of our acquaintance keeps one pair each of cordon bleus, fire finches, star finches, cherry finches, bichenos, and lavender finches in an aviary consisting of a wired-over flight twelve feet long, six feet high, and four feet wide and of a permanent shelter eight feet high, three feet long, and four feet wide. This miscellaneous group of finches does very well for him in this aviary, though, of course, there are occasional quarrels for the possession of favorite nesting and roosting sites. Incidentally, all the birds were placed in this aviary at one and the same time so that, at first, it was new to all of them and not to just some of them.

Since different varieties of birds react differently to given aviary conditions and surroundings, their keeper must be prepared to experiment in order to find out what kinds and what numbers of birds he *may* keep together harmoniously in a given enclosure. Assuredly, nobody, not even an acknowledged authority on a given species of bird, can tell in advance how a given pair of breeders will act when first placed in an aviary with other birds. Usually the best way is to put *all members* of a mixed collection in the aviary at the same time; then all of them will have to get used to the new conditions together, with none having any special advantage over any other, as would be the case were the birds introduced into the aviary pair by pair over a period of time.

In this matter it is well to keep in mind that there are few hard and fast rules governing the behavior in captivity of such lively beings as birds. Each and every bird has an individuality all its own. Its behavior in an aviary has to be studied carefully to determine the conditions under which the bird is most likely to thrive.

Another important consideration has to do with mixing in one aviary various kinds of finches, or other species, for breeding purposes, which ordinarily is not advisable. And yet, if but few pairs of birds be kept in a very spacious enclosure, the birds may get along nicely with one another, may even nest successfully. However, to insure success from the very start, it is usually best to keep each variety in a separate pen. Moreover, some varieties, as, for instance, the Gouldian finch, usually breed well only if kept with their own kind, and not with other birds.

Before building any sort of aviary, the bird fancier should decide as definitely as he can on the number and the varieties of birds he plans to keep, and whether they are to be kept simply for pleasure or also for breeding (and possible profit). He should then build a sufficient number of aviaries to fit this initial need of his, at the same time making at least some practical provision for possible additions to his collection.

Speaking generally, the same type of aviary may be used to accommodate canaries or finches or softbills or parrot-like birds or doves; that is to say, a wired-over flight and a solid, well roofed, permanent shelter are prime requisites for the protection of all birds in captivity. Of course, size and weight of aviary wire used and the interior equipment and fixtures needed will differ with the types of birds kept. These practical details will be discussed in a later chapter. Suffice it to say at this point that a reasonably roomy, substantial, and well constructed aviary would be suitable for almost any species of bird, whether hardbill or softbill. If there is the least likelihood that the fancier will keep small as well as large birds, hardbills as well as softbills, not to mention doves, quail, and the like, he should build his aviaries so that he can use them interchangeably at any time he wants to—without each time having to make important and time-consuming alterations. In other words, it pays to standardize the wired-in flights and the roofed-over shelters as to size, kind of wire netting, flooring, and other, similar essentials so that birds may be quickly and safely transferred from one aviary to another at any time. Furthermore, having wire-flights and shelters of similar, if not equal, size provides a harmonious appearance and set-up for the entire group of aviaries. Such attractive outside aviary facilities you will find in most zoological gardens, where more or less uniform flights and shelters make possible the shifting of birds from one aviary to another conveniently and quickly.

Birds of various kinds may be safely kept in outdoor aviaries in almost any sort of climate. However, as is well known, most aviary birds do best in a reasonably warm, though not very dry, climate. This applies particularly to birds whose native habitats lie in tropical regions with humid climates. Experience in aviculture has taught us that most captive birds need to be protected against continued dampness and damp cold. The outdoor aviary, therefore, must be provided with a solid shelter, a permanent structure, which is thoroughly dry and draft-proof, and one in which the birds may be conveniently fed and cared for in bad weather. Many varieties of birds, except perhaps certain tropical species, are not bothered by cold weather, provided it is not a wet cold and provided also that they have a cozy, dry shelter in which they may take refuge both day and night.

Permanent shelters or houses, equipped with windows and doors, usually adjoin the wire-flights of the aviaries. Their fronts, facing the flights, may be of the open or the closed type, the latter being customarily used in regions with cold winter climates. The closed type of house has a door leading into the flight, the upper part of which may consist of an easily manipulated window or other opening through which the birds can enter and leave the shelter at will. During inclement weather this opening is usually closed and also during the night.

Some fanciers make it a practice to chase their birds into the shelter for the night, as otherwise they would sleep outdoors and so be subject to a severe drop in temperature and to catching cold. In other words, the birds are shut up for the night, and also on very cold or wet days, thus insuring their comfort during such critical times.

Detailed descriptions of permanent shelters or houses will be given in a later chapter of this book. Suffice it to say here that wood, brick, cement, and other materials are used in their construction, depending on how permanent and lasting the shelter is meant to be and what climatic hazards it will have to withstand. Since many birds suffer from the effects of intense summer heat, any shelter worthy of its name, whether of wood or stone construction, must provide an ample amount of fresh air—must, in other words, be equipped with a sufficient number of ventilations for use in summer as well as in winter.

Since the shelter or house is really the most essential part of any aviary, usually the birds' only refuge in extemely hot or cold weather, it should be planned with special care for their well-being in all seasons and in all kinds of temperature. Thus, the rather simple  wooden type of open-front shelter attached to wire-flights customarily found in sections of the country enjoying mild winter climates would in Eastern, Mid-Western, and Southwestern regions of this country have to be replaced by a solidly built brick or stone house, which could be kept fairly cool in summer and fairly warm in winter without too much trouble or expense. In other words, adaptation of the sheltered portion of the aviary to local climatic conditions is of the utmost importance so far as the welfare of the birds is concerned.

# III

## *Important Requirements To Be Considered Before You Build Your Aviary*

An aviary may be defined as being a sizeable outdoor enclosure, usually, though not always, consisting of a wired-over or glassed-in flight with or without adjoining house or permanent shelter. Since most aviaries are built to suit their owners' special requirements as to available space, location, as well as the numbers and varieties of birds to be kept in them now or later on, no so-called standard size or sizes, as might be true if they were manufactured in quantities like cages, exist in the United States today. In other words, each birdkeeper builds an aviary to fit his own special needs and tastes. In view of the fact that these needs and tastes differ greatly, one finds in actual practice a surprising variety of shapes, sizes, locations, and combinations of flight and shelters. Whatever qualities an American built aviary may or may not possess, it can usually boast of having individuality, that individuality being even more valuable to the birds than it is to the aviary's owner.

When it comes to actual size, an aviary (including flight and house) may extend from comparatively few, let us say six, to as many as twenty and more feet in length. *Length*, sometimes referred to as depth, is highly desirable in order to afford the birds ample flying space, since vigorous and frequent wing-exercise is most certainly conducive to producing healthy and sturdy bodies. The longer the aviary, the farther its occupants can fly, and the better for them. If, therefore, you have the necessary space and the financial means

available, then by all means give your birds as much room within which to fly as possible. Moreover, the longer the flight, the more readily can one bird get out of the way of other birds, or of their keeper, without injury to itself or to others. A successful fancier of finches, siskins, and canaries breeds one pair of each of these species in an aviary consisting of a twelve-foot-long flight and a three-foot-long covered shelter. The fact that his birds have such an ample amount of space in which to fly contributes in large measure not only to their being in such excellent physical condition and perfect plumage  but also to their raising nest after nest of sturdy youngsters each season. Specific measurements for various aviaries will be furnished in a later chapter; suffice it to say here that considerable length or depth is highly desirable in any aviary.

*Height* in an aviary is important owing to the fact that most birds naturally like to fly up and also to roost as well as to nest in the upper portions of the enclosure. Moreover,

Pairs of siskins (facing page) and finches (star finch, right) can be successfully bred if not more than one pair of each is housed in a large aviary.

when a person enters an aviary having considerable height, let us say at least seven or eight feet, its occupants can quickly, and without being much frightened, get out of his way by simply flying up instead of being forced to dash against the sides of the aviary at the risk of injuring themselves. Some birdmen, however, prefer their wired-in flights not to exceed six to eight feet in height, that being in their experience the most convenient height for catching the birds with a net in the daytime, for to reach higher than eight feet would be rather awkward and ineffective. Many fanciers, who regard catching birds with nets as being rather cruel at best, prefer to catch theirs by flashlight at night when the birds have gone to roost. Incidentally, and this is important from the viewpoint of height, experienced birdkeepers have found that birds are much more likely to roost during the day or the night in the covered shelter or house that is several feet *higher* than the adjoining flight—they like to fly up into this shelter.

In actual practice many aviaries are ten, fifteen, even twenty feet high. Considerable height, it should be added, is usually appreciated by all kinds of birds, except those living mainly on the ground. Of course, the higher—and the longer—your aviary, the more materials and labor will be needed for its building, but if you can at all afford these items—and if you have the room, then by all means build as extensive a bird enclosure as possible, since it will enable you to add to your collection of birds at any time without each time running the risk of crowding them and so making them unhappy and uncomfortable. Some birdkeepers will fence in portions of their gardens or backyards including shrubs and trees, thus providing excellent keeping facilities for their birds.

Many a bird enthusiast, thinking that he will always be content with but few birds, starts out modestly with a very small and cramped aviary only to realize to his chagrin in a short time that it is inadequate to accommodate at all comfortably the more or less steadily and rapidly growing collection of which he himself is growing fonder and prouder by the day. The result is either more or less injurious crowding of his birds in the available space, or the building of additional and more spacious pens to house his growing collection adequately, at the same time providing satisfactory accommodations for more or less sudden additions to it.

While sufficient length and height are the most essential spatial requirements of your aviary from the viewpoint of giving your birds plenty of flying and breeding space, width is of lesser importance. It is, however, important from the standpoint of proportion—a well-proportioned aviary looks attractive. Like length and height, width must often be suited to the available space. And when that space happens to be narrow, harmonious proportions may have to be sacrificed.

Very narrow, less than three feet wide, aviaries, consisting of a number of flights placed in a row side by side, may offer birds an opportunity to get at one another through the wire netting, with possible injury to themselves. Parrot-like birds will sometimes bite the toes off birds in adjoining pens simply by reaching through the wire netting. Such trouble may usually be avoided from the very start by using a very small-sized mesh of wire, such as quarter-inch, for the partitions between the various pens or flights, or else one can use two sets of netting in place of the usual one; or, finally, to make absolutely sure of the birds' safety, one can use a solid material for the partitions. Pet and poultry supply houses usually stock various kinds and grades of translucent plastic and glass-covered wire netting, which has the added advantage of making it impossible for the occupants of one flight or pen to see—and, of course, to bother—those in the adjoining flight or flights. Before deciding on flight and other aviary partitions most suitable for his birds, the aviary builder should first inquire at local pet and poultry equipment houses as to what manner of materials are available, with a view to inspecting them carefully and determining their suitability for his particular needs. The extra cash outlay entailed by the purchase of such permanent materials is quickly and readily offset by the increased comfort and safety given to the birds for as long as they remain in the aviary.

If there is a choice of *locations* for your aviary, use the one in which your birds will enjoy the most and the best light and fresh air and suffer the least from the effects of unfavorable summer or winter weather. Most birds do well in a moderate climate with a temperature that is neither too hot nor too cold. They should, therefore, have suitable protection against excessive summer heat and winter cold, also against the devastating rain, wind, and dust storms to which some sections of this country are subject more or less periodically.

Since most birds like to bask in the morning sunshine, it is well to build your aviary so that its flight or other "open" portion will receive the full benefit of the morning sunlight. Afternoon sun is often too hot and enervating, especially so in the summertime. Furthermore, many birds are wont to rest in the afternoon, whereas they are most active and lively in the morning hours. At any rate, whether you use an eastern, southern, or other exposure for your aviary depends mainly on the direction from which in your particular locality you get *the least bad weather*—rainstorms, winds, etc. It is in this direction that your flights and aviaries should preferably face to afford your birds the largest measure of protection from the effects of the weather.

*Shade* is essential for your birds' comfort and general wellbeing. If, therefore, you can locate your aviary under or near some shade-giving trees, by all means do so. The relief from summer heat thus afforded your birds is an absolute necessity for them, unless, of course, you can offer them other means for keeping comfortable on hot summer days, such as excellent air-circulation, cooling sprays of water fountains, and the like. Shelters built of wood get very hot and stuffy in regions of the country such as the East, Mid-West, and others that usually have high summer temperatures, unless they are naturally or artificially shaded to reduce the temperature and so prevent the birds from getting overheated. An aviary should be placed in such a position that the birds will get the maximum of winter sunshine. That again does not imply that it must be placed in such a way that the sun can glare down on the birds at midday on the hottest summer day without their being able to find any protection for themselves. Birds love sunshine, but many people who are not fanciers at all will have noticed that in the full heat of a summer day birds seem to disappear. They like to get into the shade for a time, and many of them rest for perhaps an hour or more in the middle part of the day. Nevertheless sunshine must be available, even if protection against it when it is extreme also has to be considered.

Of course, the ideal way of providing shade is to have shrubs and small trees growing in your aviary, that is, in the flights, so that the birds may sit in the natural shade thus fur-

30

nished them. Such plantings are desirable only for aviaries in which not too many canaries, finches, siskins, or soft-bills are kept; otherwise the birds will not only soil the leaves of the plants but will very soon eat the leaves off them, leaving the plantings bare and ugly. In large aviaries with much greenery there is, of course, less danger of this sort. Since parrot-like birds will almost invariably gnaw the bark off any twigs or branches within their reach, it is not advisable to use permanent plantings of shrubs or trees in their enclosures, since they will ruin them within a very short time.

Occasionally, a bird fancier finds that small and large potted plants will give his aviary or birdroom the desired natural look. Since such plants may be moved about readily, they can, when they are no longer fresh and green, be quickly and easily replaced, thus keeping up the natural and attractive appearance of the aviary. A simple and practical way of shading an aviary from the outside is to plant climbing vines or roses along the sides. Gourds thus planted to run over the wire-flights of canary and finch aviaries will attract aphids, which in turn are much relished by most finches, which get them through the wire netting.

Three slopes for proper floor drainage: Top: High outer edge sloping to center drain; Middle: High center sloping to outside on two sides; Bottom: Entire floor sloping to one side where a trough may carry water to a drain.

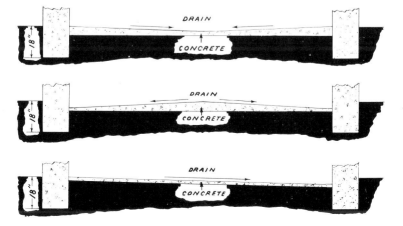

Following is a list of some plants that have desirable characteristics that make them suitable for use in aviaries:

Balsam Fir (*Abies balsamea*)-juv.
Subalpine Fir (*Abies lasiocarpa*)-juv.
White Fir (*Abies concolor*)-juv.
Douglas Fir (*Pseudotsuga menziesii*)-juv.
Eastern Hemlock (*Tsuga canadensis*)-juv.
Black Spruce (*Picea mariana*)-juv.
Red Spruce (*Picea rubens*)-juv.
White Spruce (*Picea glauca*)-juv.
Norway Spruce (*Picea abies*)-juv.
Tamarack (*Larix laricina*)-juv.
Eastern White Pine (*Pinus strobus*)-juv.
Western White Pine (*Pinus monticola*)-juv.
Spruce Pine (*Pinus glabra*)-juv.
Virginia Pine (*Pinus virginiana*)-juv.
Ponderosa Pine (*Pinus ponderosa*)-juv.
Austrian Pine (*Pinus nigra*)-juv.
Scotch Pine (*Pinus sylvestris*)-juv.
Northern White Cedar (*Thuja occidentalis*)
Chinese or Oriental Cedar (*Thuja orientalis*)
Hiba arborvitae (*Thujopsis dolobrata*)
Arizona Cypress (*Cupressus arizonica*)-juv.
Common Juniper (*Juniperus communis*)
Rocky Mountain Juniper (*Juniperus scopulorum*)
Drooping Juniper (*Juniperus flaccida*)
Eastern Red Cedar (*Juniperus virginiana*)
Black Willow (*Salix nigra*)-juv.
Pacific Willow (*Salix lasiandra*)-juv.
Peachleaf Willow (*Salix amyglaloides*)-juv.
White Poplar (*Populus alba*)-juv.
American Holly (*Ilex opaca*)
English Holly (*Ilex aquifolium*)
Common Privet (*Ligustrum vulgare*)
Spirea-species (*Sorbaria*)
Coralberry (*Symphoricarpo orbiculatus*)

When a number of budgerigars are kept together in the same aviary the cocks will court hens other than their own mates. The hens do not always reject these attentions, so the color breeders would be well advised not to keep different colors together in an aviary.

Snowberry (*Symphoricarpo albus*)
English Ivy (*Iledera helix*)
Bladdernut (*Staphylea trifolia*)
Common Elderberry (*Sambucus canadensis*)
European Elderberry (*Sambucus nigra*)
Red Elderberry (*Sambuscus pubens*)
Hawthorn-species (*Crataegus*)-juv.
Raspberries (*Rubus*)
Multiflora Rose *(Rosa multiflora)*
European Beech *(Fagus sylvatica)* - juv. or hedge
American Beech *(Fagus grandifolia)* - juv. or hedge
Prunus-species
Mock-Orange-species (*Philadelphus*)
Viburnum-species
All Huckleberries, Bilberries and relatives
(Gaylussaciae, Vacciniums)
Whin (*Genista tinctoria*)
Firethorn (*Cotoneaster pyracantha*)

If the section of the country in which you live is subject to many and heavy rains, thunder, dust, or other storms, you may wish to roof over your flights with plasti-glass or other similar material and also enclose some or all sides with the same substance. The additional cost incurred by such protection is readily offset by the reduction in losses of young and of old birds usually suffered during heavy storms. After all is said and done, most birds are rather delicate creatures— little bundles of soft feathers—and must consequently be protected from the effects of hazardous weather conditions. The right time to provide for such safeguard is *before* damage is likely to occur—at the time when you are planning and building your birdhouse.

Although many birds show no inclination during storms to seek protection in the shelter or house portion of the aviary, they may have to be given some protection also in the wire-flights, where they will be safe from the effects of excessive heat, rain, wind, and cold. Thus the top of the flight may be covered solidly in part or in whole with a transparent or other roof.

In exposed places it is unwise to have the flight covered with wire netting on all three sides. If it is known that prevailing cold winds come from a particular quarter, that side of the flight should be boarded up. In fact, there is probably much to be said for at least one side, if not two, being completely covered. It is a mistake, however, to cover the top completely, for it is of great value to birds not only to have direct sunshine but also to be able occasionally to let rain fall on their feathers. Very few birds like to remain out in a downpour, so to save them having to retire into the shelter, a small portion of the flight near the shelter can be roofed over.

To be strictly honest in this matter, however, it ought to be stated that there are breeders of considerable experience who will not under any circumstances have any part of the flight covered at all. The beginner will naturally learn from experience which method of protection he finds more satisfactory in practice, but it will do no harm to start off with part of the flight covered.

Once you have decided on the size of your aviary and on its location, your next important step concerns the kind of flooring likely to be most serviceable. If your soil has fast drainage and is in no way contaminated, you may want to use an earthen floor, which has the advantage of being both natural and inexpensive. To prevent any sort of contamination over a period of years, you should dig up the soil once or twice a year and sprinkle the top with lime, or you can renew the top layer once a year or oftener, replacing it with several inches of fresh washed river or ocean sand. In order to prevent mice, rats, and other marauders from digging through the earthen floor from the outside, cement walls should be sunk eighteen inches deep or deeper as foundations for your

Cockatiels, *(Nymphicus hollandicus)* are strong flyers, so they must be kept in a long flight which provides opportunity for enough wing exercise. In this photo the female perches at the entrance of the nest just prior to the commencement of egg-laying.

In an aviary budgerigars will breed practically the whole year through, although late autumn and winter are not suitable times for nesting. Many breeders put the starting date in February or March and end in early August.

A healthy pair of cockatiels can usually be relied on to produce three to four broods during one season. Six or even more eggs are laid to one clutch. A large wooden nest block must be hung in a sheltered part of the aviary. In this photo the male regurgitates food from the crop and prepares to feed its begging offspring.

(Left) The gold-mantled rosella *(Platycercus eximus cecilinae)* of Queensland and New South Wales (Australia) likes to live in a long aviary with a shed for roosting purposes. They can be kept with small birds (finches, canaries) but become aggressive towards other parrakeets. (Right) The Stanley rosella *(Platycercus icterotis icterotis)* breeds freely in a large aviary. A pair should be kept separately. The nestboxes must be hung in the open flight. There has to be a choice in nestboxes!

aviary, all around the flights and the shelter. An additional precaution taken by some builders is to set a *smooth-sided* wall, about twenty-four inches high, atop the cement wall, which prevents mice and other animals from climbing up on the sides of the aviary. Such precautions are well worth the extra cost of labor and materials since later on they will save endless work and bother occasioned by having to trap or to poison mice, etc., that have somehow or other gained entrance into the aviary.

Perhaps the most useful and popular kind of material to serve for aviary flooring is concrete. It furnishes sure protection against various vermin and is easily cleaned with hose and water. However, the floor should be sloped to provide proper drainage. It may be covered with a heavy layer of sand or wood shavings which will absorb moisture from droppings and other sources, this material to be renewed at more or less regular intervals. In those parts of the country in which much damp and wet weather prevails at certain seasons of the year, it would be impractical to use bare concrete floors. Since birds alighting and sitting on such cold floors frequently contract chills, it is best to use a heavy layer of sand, sawdust, peat moss, or other soft and absorptive material over the concrete. A thoroughly dry floor is highly essential to the birds' health in summer and in winter.

Another material commonly used for the floors of aviaries is thoroughly seasoned, tight-fitting, smooth wood—the tongue-and-groove kind. There are some bird fanciers who like their aviaries to have a double flooring. They place a wooden floor six or more inches above a concrete floor, in this way furnishing extra protection against mice and rats coming through from the bottom and at the same time providing good circulation of air between the two floors. The space between may be made sufficiently high to permit cats to hunt mice there. The smooth wooden floor may be left bare, in which case it should be scraped and cleaned frequently, or it may be covered with fine sand, sawdust, or other thoroughly dry and absorptive material. One fancier covers the floor of her aviary with newspapers which she renews every morning.

The choice of flooring to be used for the flights or for the shelters of an aviary, or both, depends largely on how permanently, securely, and comfortably the builder plans to keep his feathered charges. In the long run the concrete floor, perhaps the most expensive from the monetary standpoint, proves to be the least costly since it requires in most cases no repairs or other alterations during its long, useful life. If covered with suitable material, a concrete floor may be kept reasonably dry even in the wintertime when dampness and cold threaten.

Roofs for the permanent shelter may be made of shingles, tile, sheet metal, or heavy (40 or 60 lbs.) roofing paper. The kind of material used depends on how permanent the house is to be and what weather conditions it has to endure. Obviously, in sections of the country which are subject to heavy falls of rain and snow, very substantially built and strongly sloping roofs are required to withstand the sudden pressure of heavy loads of water or snow, or both. Other sections of the country, subject to severe wind and sand storms, may require heavy sheet metal roofs, which even a strong wind cannot easily dislodge.

To avoid flooding the floors of the flights adjoining the permanent shelters, the roofs should be equipped with gutters so designed as to take the water away from the enclosures. Underneath sloping roofs properly equipped with ventilators birds frequently find excellent shelter for roosting and nesting. In fact, when birds are kept in a single more or less circular structure combining flight and shelter, with one or more sides open (made of wire netting or glass), the space underneath the steeply sloping roof serves as permanent shelter and is thus equipped with roosts and nesting boxes.

As already emphasized, in aviaries having flights with ad-

The Swainson's or rainbow lorikeet *(Trichoglossus haematodus moluccanus)* of Australia and Timor can be housed in an outdoor aviary throughout the year, although adequate shelter should be available. During the winter slight heat is advisable. These birds are intolerant with other large parrots, so they should be kept separately in pairs.

Bourke's parrakeet *(Neophema bourkii)* of central Australia is a very easy to manage beautiful and well-known bird. It can be housed in a medium-sized outdoor aviary and will live in peace with small finches and softbills. During the winter an adequate frost-free shelter must be provided.

The plum-head parrakeet *(Psittacula cyanocephala)* of India and Ceylon can be kept in a medium-sized aviary when acclimatized. It is very tolerant towards other birds (finches and other parrakeets), but a pair should be offered an aviary to themselves for breeding purposes.

joining shelters, the roofs on the shelters should be raised several feet above the tops (roofs) of the flights, thus giving the birds an opportunity to fly up into the shelters and to roost high up underneath the sloping roof.

So as to prevent cats and other marauders from disturbing the birds in the wire-flights, especially during the night, a second wire netting may be stretched ten inches or higher over the first. It should preferably be of rather small mesh to keep sparrows and other undesirable guests from getting through it. Cats may also be kept off the top of flights by simply nailing a piece of heavy and stiff wire netting flat on top of the frame all around and so as to project approximately ten inches from the edges. No cat can climb over this projecting netting.

One of the bugbears that the bird-keeper has to endure is the presence of rats and mice. Wherever there are seed-eating birds, in a comparatively short space of time both these pests will put in an appearance. Rats are particularly unpleasant and can cause serious harm to birds of almost any size. In fact, it is very likely that if rats get into either the shelter or the flight, some of the inmates will be killed. They must therefore be kept out at all costs. Although that advice may sound comparatively easy to achieve, it is by no means so unless one takes very careful precautions. Naturally rats cannot get through 4 inches of concrete, so an aviary which has this depth of concrete under the flight and also under the shelter is more or less immune to them. But, even so, the bird-keeper has to keep his eye on the woodwork of shelter and flight to see that this is not attacked, because even if one of these rodents does not get in the first night, if it has started to make a hole it will certainly gain entrance during the second night—and the consequences may be disastrous.

If the floor is not made of concrete, then other precautions are necessary, and the only thing to do is to fringe both shelter and flight with wire netting to a depth of at least 2 feet. This means digging a trench of sufficient depth and also wide enough to allow the wire netting to be bent outwards. The rats then, burrowing down, will come in contact with the wire and in all probability will not be able to get through before the hole in the ground has been noticed and refilled with materials which rats find unpleasant (glass!).

Mice, although they are not as dangerous, can be a very great nuisance and are even more difficult to keep out of the aviary. Mice can, with ease, squeeze their way through wire netting of ½-in. mesh, and small mice can get through even the smallest mesh which is generally available, in fact, as small as three-eighths-in. However, every attempt must be made to keep mice out, particularly when breeding operations are in progress, for although they are not likely to injure adult birds, they will, without doubt, frighten them and, if they get into a nest, may kill or turn out the babies which are not yet fledged. Adult birds which are scared at night often do themselves serious injury by dashing into the wooden walls.

The bird-keeper is always at his wits' end in trying to prevent mice from getting into either the shelter or the flight, and it is only by persistence that finally he becomes reasonably successful. Mice find it extremely difficult to run up glass, and sheet metal presents a similar difficult foothold. Thus, if the bottom of the flight is surrounded by sheets of metal to a height of 12 to 15 in., there is every chance of success in keeping these little pests outside. One also has to bear in mind the fact that if mice do get in from time to time they must be prevented from reaching the food pots. To achieve this object all pots, whether containing food or water, should be placed on stands with flat and projecting tops. Such stands can be supported by a central post, and if the board on which the pots rest is about 2 ft. square, no mice will ever get on to the top unless they drop down on to it from the roof. Surprising as it may seem, they can do this, and then later jump several feet to the ground without injuring themselves in the least.

Peach-faced lovebirds *(Agapornis roseicollis)* from East Africa carry bits of bark between the feathers on the back to the nestboxes. The birds should be put in pairs in an aviary during the breeding season, as they are fierce fighters among themeselves.

**OPPOSITE:** masked lovebirds *(Agapornis personata)* from northeastern Tanzania can be kept in pairs, but there is a risk of young birds being attacked and/or injured in the nests, so providing a small aviary and keeping the birds in single couples in each compartment can help to solve the problem. The birds will fill up their nestboxes with fresh willow bark.

A very practical feature found in many an aviary is the double door. It is used to prevent birds from escaping when their keeper enters or leaves the aviary. Any birds escaping from the aviary proper through the main door are trapped in the small vestibule containing the second door and are easily caught there. So that all aviary doors may shut quickly, they should be provided with springs.

An almost indispensable convenience in a birdhouse is electric lighting, both inside and outside of the house. It is especially appreciated by the birdkeeper on gloomy days or dark mornings when necessary chores must be done in the aviary. A powerful light may be placed at such a height outside the aviary as to light up a whole group of pens from the top at night. Nocturnal marauders may thus be quickly discovered and turned away. Electric bulbs placed within the aviary should be covered with a wire screen to prevent the birds from coming into direct contact with them.

*Warmth* may be supplied to the birds in the wintertime by means of radiators, hot water pipes, or thermostatically controlled electric heaters. The thicker and the more insulated the walls of the birdhouse, the freer it is from draft and dampness, and consequently the less need exists for supplying artificial heat, which ordinarily should not exceed sixty degrees. Heat produced by open gas flame or smoking oil lamps is likely to prove injurious to birds and should therefore not be used. Even parrot-like birds have been kept in good health in the wintertime in unheated but solidly built brick and stone houses. Some tropical birds, however, like golden fronted fruitsuckers, honey creepers, tanagers, sunbirds, and numerous others require some artificial heat on cold winter days and nights. It is highly essential that birds kept in heated aviaries and rooms be supplied with plenty of fresh air; otherwise they soon become dull and listless. Moreover, if the heated air lacks humidity, the birds' plumage loses its lustre and life, with the individual feathers becoming dry and brittle. Humidity may simply be supplied by letting a pan of boiling water evaporate slowly in some part of the aviary where the birds will not come into direct contact with it. A small fountain playing in the aviary and emitting a fine spray of water provides humidity aplenty.

Insulation against dampness as well as cold may be provided by using double walls, stuffing rockwool or other suitable insulating material in between them. Painting both outside and inside walls of the aviary several coats is a simple but effective means of insulating. Paints containing lead should ordinarily be avoided for the inside walls since some birds are wont to gnaw and eat particles of the painted wood. Of course, the paint should be thoroughly dry before any birds are placed in the aviary. Nowadays many special insulating and inexpensive wallboards are offered on the market, which the aviary builder will do well to investigate. For their products the various manufacturers of wallboards claim a high degree of protection against heat, cold, dampness, as well as sound. Insulating wallboard is made in convenient sizes for quick and ready use, even by the amateur builder. Its use provides coolness in summer and warmth in winter for the birdhouse, thus assuring its occupants of continuing comfort and well-being.

Naturally the flight provides no ventilation problem, but the shelter requires well-thought-out ventilation with an inlet low down and protected against mice, and an outlet on the opposite wall near the eaves. By careful thought this inlet and outlet can be so arranged that there is no possibility of the birds' being in a draft, but it is most important that on hot summer days there should be free current of air through the shelter. This is perhaps even more important at night when all the birds will be in the shelter. It is also an advantage, too, to have windows that open. The window spaces must be protected by wire netting so that the birds cannot escape.

At all times glass must be covered with ½-in. wire netting, because birds cannot see glass and will fly into it head-first

The halfmoon or Petz's conure *(Aratinga canicularis eburnirostrum)* (above, left) is sold mainly as a pet "dwarf parrot." The sexes are particularly difficult to determine. A good pet halfmoon is really a delightful bird, and youngsters are reasonably easy to train. Though halfmoons can thrive in an aviary only four feet long, the ideal length is sixteen feet—that is, sixteen feet of straight, unimpaired flying space. A pair of cactus conures *(Aratinga c. cactorum)* from Brazil (above, right) can better be kept in a small aviary by themselves, as the cock sometimes will attack all other parrakeets during the breeding time. Tovi parrakeets *(Brotogeris jugularis jugularis)* (below) from Colombia and Central America are very sociable, so they like other birds in their aviary. They should always be kept in pairs.

Nest and eggs. A typical canary's nest built in a 'nest pan.' The usual clutch is three to five eggs, and occasionally hens will produce only an odd egg or two, or lay big clutches of seven or eight. The hen generally starts to incubate after the first or second egg, and in a clutch of five it will mean a difference in age between the youngsters of three to four days. As each egg is laid it should be removed to an egg box and replaced in the nest by an imitation pot egg. When the full clutches have been laid the real eggs can all be replaced under the respective hens. The incubation period is thirteen to fourteen days. Should a breeder wish to keep canaries solely for the purpose of 'decoration' and song, an aviary is ideal accommodation. The majority of canaries are bred in cages, but some breeds are successfully raised in small indoor pens. Canaries cannot stand excessive dampness or drafts. Good ventilation is essential for good health.

This small garden aviary, designed by Carl Papp, embodies all the principles of efficient planning to meet requirements for finches and delicate softbills. The safety door prevents escapes. The inside shelter has fitted panels on the front to protect the birds at night or in bad weather. During the day the panels are removed, but no draft can enter. The planted outside flight is accessible by a sliding window which can be closed from outside the flight when the birds are to be enclosed in the shelter. The glass is frosted so that it is visible as a barrier, thereby preventing headlong crashes against the pane. An opaque panel could be used in its place, but the frosted glass admits light when the protective panels on the front of the aviary are in place.

and do themselves considerable damage unless it is made visible to them.

The space through which the birds enter the shelter from the flight is sometimes called the pophole. Occasionally the word 'bobhole' is used.

It is essential that the birds should spend the night in the shelter, and when they are unaccustomed to their surroundings, the task of getting them in is not always easy. For this reason a good deal of thought has to be paid both to the situation and to the size of the pophole. It is not unusual, during the first few days after a number of fresh birds have been introduced, to have to drive them into the shelter at night, and this can be a very difficult job indeed. Behaving from what can only be instinct, they always try to get as high up as possible. Normally popholes are not put right at the top of the division between the flight and the shelter, but it is an excellent idea to have a hole here, either as a temporary measure in addition to the ordinary bobhole or, if one wishes it, as a permanent part of the arrangement of the aviary. Certainly it is far less trouble to get birds in when the entrance is right at the very top.

If birds which have been living in an aviary for some time are disinclined to go into the shelter, that is almost certainly due to the fact that the shelter is not light enough. Birds object very strongly to going into the dark, and so it is of great importance that a shelter should be light enough to attract them. It should be so light, in fact, that they do not notice any real difference between the conditions in the flight and those in the shelter into which they are expected to retire at the coming of dusk.

There are various devices which can be used to shut the pophole through which the birds go in and out from the shelter to the flight, but by far the simplest from the point of view of the operator is one which can be manipulated without having to go into the aviary at all. It will not tax the ingenuity of the handyman, and certainly not of the aviary manufacturer, to produce a slide which can be pushed across to close the entrance when all the birds have gone in safely for the night.

Young canaries. A nest of chicks at about ten days old gaping for food. For the first few days it is advisable not to bother the hen with her youngsters beyond giving them their food, greens and, of course, their water.

The evening before the chicks are due to be hatched some soft food should be given to the parents so that they can be fully prepared to feed their young when they arrive. Numerous, well-balanced rearing foods are obtainable already mixed, with full instructions for their use.

# Aviary Fittings and Fixtures

So far as the interior fittings and furnishings of your aviary are concerned, they would ordinarily include perches, nesting arrangements, feeders, drinkers, and other essentials that you can either buy at your local pet shop or, if you are at all handy with hammer and saw, you can make them yourself and have a lot of fun besides. In providing this equipment, aim at simplicity and usefulness.

Carefully note how your birds react to the perches, nest boxes, and other necessary facilities you provide for them. If they do not use them readily or in a way that is conducive to their welfare, do not hesitate to make such changes as will insure the full and proper use of this equipment. By no means clutter up the inside of your birdhouse with a lot of useless, artificial gadgets which soon gather dust and dirt and which often lend the aviary an unreal and artificial atmosphere wholly unsuited to birdkeeping. The simpler your aviary is furnished, the more room in which to fly and cavort its occupants will have, and the more natural it is likely to look. After all is said and done, whenever you look inside your aviary, you want to see and to enjoy the birds, not a lot of needless equipment that is in the way of your birds and yourself. Birds are nature's very own creatures, and they like being kept in as simple and natural surroundings as possible.

## SPARE EQUIPMENT

A certain amount of spare equipment is absolutely essential unless one is prepared to find oneself in difficulty from time to time, for there will certainly be breakages of food and water pots and other articles of equipment also. Even the cages and flights in the shelters will need to be repaired and renewed from time to time.

Therefore, it is certainly a help to have a number of spare feeding and water pots, to say nothing of the baths which will be used in the various cages and aviaries or the separate flight compartments in the shelter.

It is a practical idea to have baths of different colors, for some birds seem to have a fear of bathing in white pots. They prefer brown. Others are quite happy to go into a dish which is made of glass, but if there is a variety of colors, the needs of all the birds one is likely to keep will be satisfied.

The bird-keeper who has all the cages and aviaries filled is asking inconvenience at some time in the future, for the day will undoubtedly come when he wants to segregate a bird for sickness or for some other reason, and he will have no cage or aviary in which to put it. There ought always to be at least one spare cage in readiness for such an emergency at all times, and if there is sufficient cash available to provide several spares, so much the better.

Sections of wire netting framed in wood will also be found useful, as occasionally sections of netting which need replacing will be noticed. By fitting over the damaged area a small section of framed wire already prepared, the complete job that has to be done later can be done when it is convenient.

## WIRE NETTING

The most widely used and most practical type of enclosure for most kinds of birds is wire netting. It may usually be had in a wide variety of sizes and weights to suit the different purposes of fanciers. Its cost depends on weight and size of mesh. To make the birds caged in by wire netting easily visible from the outside, the netting should be painted with black enamel on both sides.

The mesh used should be small enough to prevent birds from escaping through it as well as prevent mice and other animals from entering through it. For finches, netting of

Soon to leave the nest. Young Gloster fancy canaries at about eighteen days of age, only partly covered with their still-growing feathers.

56

Just independent. Two young green canaries newly weaned. It is still rather difficult to ascertain the sex of young canaries. As a general rule young cocks are more bold in appearance and livelier in action than the young hens. Young cocks are frequently seen trying to sing; young hens are usually quieter in behavior and less aggressive.

half-inch mesh serves the purpose well, while one-half or three-quarter inch mesh is customarily used for parakeets. Some fanciers prefer to use so-called window screen since it keeps flies, mosquitoes, etc., out effectively. Birds of cockatiel size usually require one-half inch or three-quarter inch netting, and the large parrots may be kept in by means of inch-and-a-half heavy so-called plaster wire or other heavy mesh, next to which, to serve as suitable partition between adjoining pens, is often placed a three-quarter or one-half inch piece of netting to prevent the birds from biting the toes and legs of the occupants in the adjoining flights. Since practically all parrot-like birds will over a period of time gnaw to pieces any wood posts and partitions at all accessible to them, such equipment should not be left bare, as it may be in finch and canary enclosures, but should be carefully covered with heavy-mesh wire netting on the inside of the aviary. Moreover, parrots, cockatoos, and macaws can, with their powerful beaks, readily bite through light-weight netting, which kind should therefore never be used for these birds' enclosures.

In case glass is used for the sides of an aviary or birdhouse, it should be covered on the inside with wire netting so as to prevent birds flying against it from breaking it and from injuring themselves. Solid walls made of glass, plasti-glass and similar modern materials have the advantage not only of keeping all undesirable guests out of the aviary but also of protecting its occupants from all hazards of weather. Most modern transparencies of this sort will give the birds the full benefit of the sun's rays.

## PERCHES

If it is your intention to keep birds which usually stay off the ground and are wont to fly about a good deal, then be sure to supply them with suitable and sufficient perches. You can buy perches at your pet shop or you can cut them yourself from tree branches. To enable the birds' feet to take a firm hold, the perches should be neither too smooth nor too rough. Natural branches make most suitable perches, since they are more or less supple, bending readily as the birds alight on them, and since they come in almost any desired thickness. When after long use they have become dry and brittle, they should be promptly replaced with fresh ones. Most perches are round, even though oval-shaped ones are also in use.

The thickness of the perch to be used depends on the variety of birds kept. Naturally, the larger the bird, the thicker and heavier the perches which he requires. Ordinarily it is advisable to supply your birds with perches *varying in thickness* so that their feet may not become cramped by having to grasp perches all of which are of the same size. A perch should not be so small in diameter as to make it necessary for the bird sitting on it to grasp it too firmly. After all, it is meant to serve as a resting place for the bird and therefore should be of sufficient thickness (diameter) to make holding on to it for dear life unnecessary.

For birds of finch, canary, and parrakeet size, perches one-half to one inch in diameter are suitable. For the larger parrot-like birds perches may vary all the way from one to two inches in diameter, and more. By giving your birds a number of perches of varying thickness, they will soon choose the ones they find most suitable and comfortable.

So far as *placement* of perches in an aviary is concerned they should be set far enough apart to give your birds as much flying exercise as possible, which condition would apply to any birds that are in the habit of flying about a good deal. To prevent birds from soiling perches, they should not be placed directly below each other. A good place for perches is along the sides of the flight and along the sides or walls of the shelter, thus leaving the birds plenty of room in the center to fly unhindered and their keeper ready access to any part of the aviary without danger of running into the perches. Fastened at varying heights in the birdhouse, perches give its occupants a choice of places at which to sit and to

The red factor canary is by far the most important of the new colors.
This red orange cock is the result of many years of work following
the introduction of red genes into the canary by crossing it with the
black-hooded red siskin *(Spinus cuculatus)*.

Brazilian crested cardinals *(Paroaria cucullata)* from South America are too large to be included with most small finches, but they do well with large, strong finches and medium softbills. In a spacious planted aviary they sing quite freely and melodiously, but in average aviaries they seldom are inclined to sing.

rest. If young or old birds unable to fly are on the floor of the aviary, it is a good plan to place some perches fairly close to the ground to enable such birds to get off it and to climb higher and higher by means of suitably placed perches.

The habits of the species of birds you keep will in large measure determine the kind of perching arrangements which you should provide. Comparatively few and well placed and spaced perches are always better than many and poorly placed ones. Keep in mind also that by putting a perch in a given location in your birdhouse, you practically compel your birds to sit there. It is obvious, therefore, that if you wish your birds to frequent a certain part of your aviary, where perhaps you can see them readily from the outside or where they will be well sheltered, you will provide perching facilities in that particular location so that your birds in turn may accommodate you.

In most cases it is not good policy to locate perches so close against the sides of a wire-flight that birds using them can bother the occupants of adjoining flights. This sort of "fraternizing" is especially to be guarded against in the case of birds kept for breeding which may thus be seriously disturbed. Parrots have been known to bite toes off the feet of birds housed in adjoining flights that stuck their toes through the wire netting. Without question, the most effectual safeguard against birds in one pen troubling those in adjoining pens is the use of solid glass or plastic or wooden partitions; wooden partitions have the added advantage of preventing birds in one pen from seeing birds in other pens. Double wire partitions are another good safeguard.

As already suggested, as perches become dry and lose their resiliency they should be promptly renewed. Mite-infested perches should be burned. Incidentally, the best protection against mites, lice, etc.—they tend to bother canaries especially—is to cresote all lumber to be used in the construction of flights and shelters, but not the perches or other sitting and roosting places.

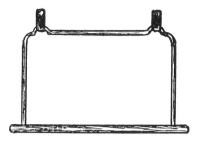

Wide double bird swing.

Spring-equipped perches.

To take some of the rigidity and hardness out of the commonly used round and dry perches, they may be wrapped with a layer of rubber or cloth, thus softening the shock to the bird as he alights on them. Such wrapping should be removed when it becomes soiled or torn. And since some types of birds will invariably tear the wrapping up and so get their feet caught in it, most birdkeepers prefer a plain round perch made elastic by means of a wire spring wrapped around the end which is to come next to the wall. The wire spring is provided with a special fastener that is readily attached to any sidewall. In other words, the perch itself does not touch the wall against which it is fastened at all, but swings clear of it on the elastic spring support. Such perches are obtainable at pet shops and worth trying out, unless, of course, one can get plenty of natural tree branches of varying thicknesses.

**Nesting Facilities**

If your aim is to have your birds produce young, then proper nesting facilities are of the utmost importance. Here again, you must cater to the natural inclinations of your birds as much as possible. Some varieties of birds use open nests placed in sheltered nooks and corners, while others prefer closed boxes provided with a hole that serves as both entrance and exit. Moreover, some birds build their own nests in part or in whole, others preferring ready-built nests.

The sulphur-breasted toucan *(Ramphastus sulphuratus)* is from the dense tropical rain forests of Central America and has a penetrating croak which can be heard half a mile away! Despite its apparent solidity, the formidable-looking bill is porous and of very light construction, and will not inflict much damage. Toucans can not stand cold, fog and damp conditions, although they become quite hardy when acclimatized. They need a large aviary with high perches. They also create havoc with most plants but are generally fairly peaceful towards larger softbills and such.

Green cardinals *(Gubernatrix cristata)* from Brazil and Argentina are excellent aviary birds and are the best breeders of the cardinals. They can be housed with other birds of similar size outside the breeding season. The female, not pictured, is much duller in color than the male, especially in the dominant black and yellow shadings.

Mynahs are totally unsuited to live in small aviaries. The lesser hill mynah *(Gracula religiosa)* from southern Asia makes a delightful pet; it becomes exceedingly tame and playful. Young birds can be taught to imitate the human voice and other sounds, as well as domestic noises (such as the creaking of door hinges!).

The nest-making habits of birds are highly individualized. Unless they are effectively catered to, birds in captivity will simply refuse to breed. In such cases their keeper will often place the blame for failure to breed on the birds when as a matter of fact it is ignorance of the birds' requirements that is the real cause of the failure.

Siskins, canaries, linnets, and some kinds of finches prefer to build their own nests in well-sheltered parts of the birdhouse, in hidden corners, under rafters, in shrubs and trees. Usually they will accept suitable opportunities in the form of wire baskets or open boxes and platforms situated in the birds' favorite nesting locations. Furnished with dry grasses, moss, small feathers, and other soft materials, the birds soon select what they need for their home building. Always their keeper should see to it that there are at least two nesting facilities for each pair of birds in order to avoid quarrels and possible destruction of nests already built. These facilities should be provided in different locations at suitable heights.

Some varieties of foreign finches, such as the zebra finch,

Wire nest for canaries.

Rack for nesting material, green food, etc.

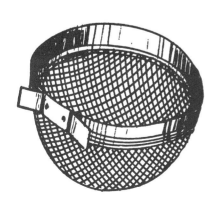

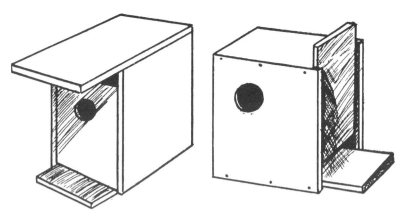

Ideal finch nest.　　　　　　　　Ideal parrakeet nestbox.

the saffron finch, and many others prefer boxes in which to
bring up their broods of young. At least two boxes are hung
up for each pair. Such boxes are procurable at any pet shop,
or else they may easily be made from lumber taken from dis-
carded light weight grocery boxes. Finch nest boxes should
be six inches high, five and one-half inches wide, and six and
one-half inches deep. The front is provided with a round
hole, one and one-half inches in diameter. The top, which
overhangs by several inches in front to shade the entrance
hole, is best hinged so that it may readily be lifted up for easy
inspection of the contents of the box. The inside bottom of
the box should be flat. Between the top or cover of the box
and the front wall, a half-inch space is left for ventilation.

Nest boxes for parrakeets, spaced as far apart in the aviary
as possible, should be from nine to ten inches high, five inches, or even six, square, with a one and one-half inch wide
entrance hole placed at least seven and one-half inches high.
Under this hole is placed a small round perch four inches
long, with approximately half of it projecting on the outside
and half on the inside of the box. For lovebirds a well-known
fancier uses a nestbox nine inches high, seven inches wide,
and six inches deep; for cockatiels the box is thirteen inches

The Java sparrow or rice bird *(Padda oryzivora)* from Indonesia can be kept in an outdoor aviary when acclimatized. They are not often aggressive and can therefore be housed with small finches and such, although they sometimes can be disturbing elements among other little birds. Hence it is preferable to keep a pair with other birds of the the same size. The white Java sparrow is a domestic variety of the rice bird.

The Pekin robin
*othrix lutea)* from the
malayas and southern
China flourishes in an
outdoor aviary. A
feeding pair, however,
ould have an aviary to
emselves, as they fre-
ently rob the nests of
er birds and even eat
the eggs!

The purple glossy starling *(Lamprotornis purpureus)* from West and Central Africa is extremely hardy and easily maintained on a standard softbilled diet. Mynah pellets are an excellent single unit food for them if the bird fancier wishes to simplify diet to the ultimate. These starlings are the easiest of the larger softbills to acclimatize. They like a large aviary and are not to be trusted in mixed company.

Having a variety of nests for finches is helpful. The grass enclosed in large wire mesh is used as a nesting site for several pairs or as a holder for dried grasses used by the birds for other nests.

high, nine inches wide and eight inches deep, with the entrance hole placed eight inches up. The boxes are placed at heights varying from six to eight feet under the shelter. Some fanciers use nest boxes with sliding bottoms for easier cleaning.

For large-sized parrots, cockatoos, and macaws, four 1 x 12" boards, six to eight feet long, may be nailed together. The entrance hole is at least six inches in diameter. No outside perch is required. However, on the inside of the front wall of the box a piece of four-inch wide hardware cloth is nailed from the bottom of the box up to the entrance hole to serve as ladder for the birds going in and out. Two nestboxes filled up to within eight inches of the entrance hole with sawdust or sand and peat moss mixed are provided for each pair of birds. The sawdust or other material is renewed in the spring of each year.

Occasionally some parrot-like birds will refuse to nest in *any* box. Thus a bird fancier found it necessary to furnish tree stumps with holes in them for some ringneck parrakeets which simply would not go into the boxes furnished them. A pair of rare black cockatoos preferred to nest on the bare ground rather than risk the dark interior of a man-made box. Large oak barrels, instead of boxes, are used by some bird keepers to serve as nesting facilities for parrots, cockatoos, and macaws. The height at which the facilities are placed in the aviary is more or less immaterial.

So far as softbilled birds and doves are concerned, they prefer to make their own nests in open wire baskets or boxes hidden in suitably sheltered locations. Many softbills, such as thrushes, flycatchers, and similar birds build very substantial nests of their own, needing no material assistance from their keeper in the form of boxes or platforms, only suitable nesting materials in the form of fine twigs, moss, small feathers, and the like. Most of these birds prefer to nest off the ground, some as high up as they can possibly get. Where open baskets and boxes are provided, care must be

The zebra finch *(Taeniopygia castanotis)* of Australia presents no problems. They are easy to house in aviaries and large cages. The species is quite domesticated and comes in a variety of colors. Therefore the zebra finch is the ideal bird for the beginner in the keeping and breeding of foreign birds. They even make excellent foster-parents.

**OPPOSITE, Upper photo:** The tri-colored mannikin *(Lonchura malacca)* from India is very easy to keep in a garden aviary. It is cheap, hardy and quite colorful. Breeding successes have, however, been few.

**OPPOSITE, Lower photo:** The black-headed mannikin *(Lonchura malacca arricapilla)* from India and Burma is quite hardy and therefore may be kept outside in winter in an aviary. The bird is friendly and tolerant towards other birds. Breeding successes are exceptional. The aviary must be well planted. The white headed mannikin *(Lonchura maja)* (right) from Indonesia is friendly and also never disturbing in a mixed collection. All mannikins like perching high up in the aviary. Their song is inaudible.

taken to place them in locations protected from wind and weather, especially the effects of glaring, hot sunlight and heavy rains.

There is one rule which is of inestimable value to all bird fanciers who are interested in breeding foreign birds. It is that once breeding has started the birds should not be interfered with at all. The temptation to look into the nest to see whether the first egg has been laid may be very great, but it is a temptation which must be resisted, for the majority of species resent interference while their breeding operations are in progress. If they are disturbed, they are very likely to desert. It is far better to wait and find out by observation whether eggs have been laid, and later whether chicks have been hatched. By standing well away from the site of the nest, one can usually tell whether the hen is sitting. If she disappears for long periods the signs are good, for it is unlikely that she has died.

There can be no doubt at all that there have been more failures in the breeding of foreign birds through the interference of the owner than from any other cause, even with those species which are reasonably free breeders.

If one is observant, it is often comparatively easy to know when the eggs have hatched, for at that time the normal thing is for both parents to be most assiduous in collecting food to take to their young, and the number of journeys they make to and from the nest will be much greater than at normal times. Some chicks give evidence of their existence by the noise they make, even a few days after they have been hatched, but others remain completely silent almost until the day when they emerge from the nest as fledglings.

There are a number of species in which the adult birds eat seed almost entirely, and for the greater part of the year are comparatively uninterested in live food, yet when they have young in the nest, they are most anxious to find live food to feed to the chicks. If they cannot find this food, the young may quickly die of starvation.

This large nest hammock is inhabited by several pairs of birds. Grass is packed in large wire mesh and suspended from the ceiling. The nests are lined with feathers and commercial nesting material. Photographed in Carl Papp's aviaries.

The easiest birds to cater to are those which feed their young entirely on seed. It may be seed which has been taken into their own crops and is regurgitated after being partially digested, or it may merely be seed which has been husked and is fed almost in its natural state.

The time that the young spend in the nest after being hatched varies very considerably from species to species. It may

The cut-throat finch *(Amadina fasciata)* from Africa likes a roomy cage or, when acclimatized, a large aviary with a shelter for use during winter. They are easy to obtain, quite free breeders, hardy and attractive. They are easy to distinguish, as only the male carries the distinctive red throat band. Cut-throat finches should not be housed for breeding with smaller or more delicate birds as both cocks and hens can become aggressive when nesting.

The male African fire finch *(Lagonostica senegala)* is a favorite member of the waxbill family and is inexpensive. It ranks alongside the cordon bleu in popularity, but it usually is a better breeder, especially when housed in a garden aviary together with other small finches. They are susceptible to low temperatures and damp.

The dusky twinspot *(Euschistos-piza cinereovinacea)* from Angola is rare in aviculture. Upper parts (not shown in this picture) are slate-black. Sexes are very much alike. Twinspots are difficult when first imported, because they will usually not accept a well rounded diet which includes insects or softbilled foods as well as live foods and seeds. This species, which can be kept in a large outdoor aviary with other finches, is closely related to Dybowski's twinspot.

The cordon bleu *(Uraeginthus bengalus)* from tropical Africa is a waxbill and one of the most popular of all the birds which fanciers call finches. Moreover, as the male in this picture shows, it is one of the most attractive. The female lacks the maroon patch on the side of the head and has less extensive blue in a quieter shade. Several pairs can be kept together in a roomy aviary, as they are far from aggressive.

be as short as ten days, it may be as long as twenty-one. The longer the birds are in the nest, the nearer they are to being independent when they emerge, but most young birds need still to be fed by their parents after they have come out of the nest, and suitable food must be provided for them at this time. It will be noticed that the young quite quickly attempt to feed themselves on the diet which will be natural to them when they are adult, but they will also rely upon what is given to them by their parents.

Sometimes the cock is difficult between the time when the young leave the nest and the age when they can fend for themselves. He may have fed the young birds extremely well while they were in the nest, but when they are outside he seems to be anxious for the hen to start to breed again, and he may not only refuse to feed the young but also may even be rough with them. If he is seen to be spiteful, the cock must be removed and the burden of feeding has to be left to the hen; it is a task which she is quite capable of performing unaided in normal circumstances.

If a further nest is required, the young can be moved to a separate compartment as soon as they are fully independent, and the cock can then be brought back to the hen.

It often happens that chicks leave the nest, are fed by their parents until they can fend for themselves without any assistance, and then begin to develop satisfactorily but do not survive until the following spring. Many attempts have been made to explain why this happens, but none of the explanations carries complete conviction. It is probable, of course, that during the period they were in the nest their feeding was inadequate  and that this fact has made them less robust when they were separated and put on their own. Perhaps even now not enough is known of the requirements of all young birds between the age when they are separated from their parents and the time when they themselves become fully adult, but as the years go by and the hobby of foreign birds and their breeding increases in scope, many of the questions which are now unanswered will be satisfactorily solved.

## Feeders and Drinkers

So far as feeders are concerned, a wide variety is in practical use nowadays. For seedeating birds, box-like hoppers in the form of so-called self-feeders with glass fronts may be obtained from pet shops. These hoppers usually hold considerable quantities of seed, sufficient for a number of days or even a week or longer. They are often divided into a series of narrow compartments, in which each kind of seed, cafeteria-style, is given separately, thus enabling the birds to make their own mixtures to suit their needs. Around the bottom of these feeders extends a detachable tray that is designed to catch, and to save for possible further use, seeds thrown aside by the birds.

Feed hoppers should, of course, be so built that the birds cannot soil their contents in any way and cannot sit or walk on the seed. Pet shops offer a good variety of feeders for various kinds of birds and in numerous different sizes and shapes. Usually it is best to place the feeders in the sheltered

Glass-fronted feeder.                    A five-hole feed hopper.

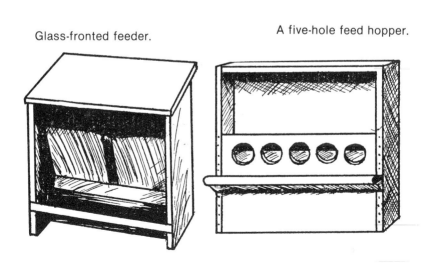

The black crowned waxbill *(Estrilda nonnula)* from central Africa is a very handsome species, but its two most attractive features do not appear in this photograph. The rump and uppertail coverts are brilliant red. The scapulars and shoulders are finely barred with alternating paler and darker shades of gray and dusky black. Although breeding this species is not always easy, many satisfactory results in large, well planted outdoor aviaries have been recorded. The birds require plenty of sunshine and small insects.

In the past years the red-headed finches *(Amadine erythrocephala)* from South Africa have frequently become available. Females lack the red on the head and the well-defined spots on the chest. This species is larger and more dominant than its relative, the cut-throat or ribbon finch. It should not, in most instances, be kept with smaller finches.

Pintailed nonpareil parrot finches *(Erythrura parasina)* (above, left) from Indonesia are sharply and beautifully colored, but the bright red underparts fade drastically in captivity. The masked grassfinches *(Poephila personata)* (above, right) from northern Australia are very peaceful and beautiful lively birds. They are very fast flyers, so they need a large outdoor aviary. These grassfinches are neither aggressive nor inquisitive. The chestnut breasted mannikin *(Lonchura castaneothorax)* (below, left) from Australia is very hardy and peaceful. The birds are difficult to sex. The dance of the male in display is the most reliable indicator. Most males have larger beaks than the females. The star finch *(Bathilda ruficauda)* (below, right) from N. Australia is a very popular finch and suited to aviary life. It is peaceful, not shy, quite hardy, a cheerful singer and a devoted parent.

This deluxe and attractive feeder has a holder on the side for green-food.

Wild bird feeders such as these are ideal in an aviary for seed or mynah pellets.

These two attractive and ornate feeders, though designed to feed wild birds, are readily adaptable to aviary use. The one on the left is best for seed, and the one on the right has a central area for mynah pellets and side areas for impaling apple and orange halves.

portion of the aviary, where it is not subject so much to the effects of the weather. Some birdmen prefer to hang the hoppers up high, out of reach of mice. Where a good many birds are kept in an aviary, it is a good plan to place a number of feeders at their disposal, putting them in different locations.

When only one feed hopper with an open tray is used, it sometimes happens that a particularly bossy bird will rule over the entire feed supply, chasing other birds away from it. However, there are feed hoppers in use so constructed that to reach the seed the bird must stick his head through one of

The rufous-necked weaver (Ploceus cucullatus), from. Africa, is an ideal aviary bird with budgerigars and medium-size hardy soft-bills.

The Senegal combassou (Hypochera chalybeata), an African whydah, is a hardy bird after it has been acclimated in an outdoor aviary with finches and small softbills. This species is generally less able to withstand damp or cold weather.

The red-billed weaver *(Quelea quelea)* is an extremely hardy bird and low in price, but it is very aggressive to small birds. These weavers are often available and very easy to take care of. They are not considered good breeders in captivity, because of their quarrelsome nature. They must have an aviary to themselves. The cock will begin to build a nest almost immediately upon being put into a well-planted garden aviary. They may be kept together with cut-throats, zebra finches and budgerigars. A daily supply of fresh grass must be available.

Male paradise whydahs *(Steganura paradisea)* from Central Africa have, in color, lavish tail feathers which never fail to attract attention. Moreover, they are peaceful with even the smallest finches and are inexpensive. Therefore they are ideal for beginners and always popular with advanced fanciers. Despite the sparrowlike drabness of females and of males in eclipse plumage, the paradise whydah is one of the most popular finches in aviculture.

a number of round holes and he is thus prevented from bothering other birds which also want to eat at the same time.

Some fanciers like to place, fresh every day, each kind of seed as well as grit and other essential extras, in open saucerlike dishes. The various dishes they set in ordinary, not too deep, grocery cartons, where the birds can readily see and find their food. By this simple device, any seeds scattered by the birds will not be strewn on the floor of the aviary or birdroom, but will be left in the various cartons, from which they may readily be removed. This practical scheme saves both feed and labor. Moreover, by means of it the birds are prevented from eating soiled or even contaminated seeds which have been thrown onto the aviary floor and have lain there for some time.

A Pacific coast fancier who has been breeding parrot-like birds successfully for many years uses what he calls a "mailbox" feeder. It simply consists of a smooth board fourteen inches long and twelve inches wide fastened to a wood post that stands three to four feet above the ground. Over the top of this post is hung an empty two-pound coffee can to prevent mice from climbing up to the feeder. The fourteen-inch long board is—mailbox-like—entirely roofed over with a piece of tin or sheet metal, the highest point of the curved tin being ten inches, leaving both ends open for the birds to enter. The seeds are simply placed in the bottom of this box with its open ends. If it develops that the birds begin to gnaw the post on which the feeder is set, then strips of tin or aluminum are nailed along the sides.

The food of softbills is usually placed in open dishes which in turn are placed on a standing or hanging table or platform. Since ants are likely to seek access to the food, it is best to smear a layer of heavy grease around the table legs to prevent them from crawling up. On hanging feeders, one smears grease on the wires by which the feeders are suspended.

86

## Drinking Facilities

Since fresh, cool water is a prime necessity for all birds kept captive, it will pay the builder of an aviary to make suitable and practical provision for a convenient and steady supply of it. Accordingly, he can have a waterpipe running lengthwise through all the flights or shelters a few inches above the floor. In each flight or shelter there is at least one small hole on the underside of the pipe which lets the water flow into a pan placed there. The water is turned on by means of a valve located at a place outside the aviary, from which the whole procedure can be seen conveniently. As soon as the waterpans are filled, which requires but a few moments, the valve is turned off. The various waterpans are shaded by means of suitable metal covers. In hot weather the water is renewed several times a day. In cold regions the waterpipes are wrapped with heavy insulating material to prevent their freezing and bursting in winter, or else their use during that season of the year is entirely discontinued and drinking water is supplied by other means.

To furnish a continuous supply of fresh water to the birds, steadily dripping faucets may be installed together with a suitable run-off for the surplus water as it overflows. In sandy soils such overflow simply soaks into the ground; in

Drinking dish.

Bath dish.

Diamond doves *(Geopelia cuneata)* from Australia are excellent and delightful additions to a finch collection housed in an outside aviary. Excellent breeders and inexpensive, these miniatures are very peaceful if no more than one pair is included in each aviary. They have to have dry sleeping quarters.

**OPPOSITE, upper photo:** Chinese painted or button quails, *(Excalfactoria chinensis,* sometimes as *Coturnix chinensis)* from Southern Asia are excellent breeders in a well-planted outdoor aviary. The male is far more colorful than the female, but both are charming and fascinating additions to any finch collection. The aviary should be provided with plenty of ground cover (tussocks of grass).

**OPPOSITE, lower photo:** The ruddy ground dove *(Columbigallina talpacoti)* ranges from Mexico to Argentina and is about six and a half inches long. The female has less brown and more gray on the upperparts and is also more gray on the underparts. This is one of a group of several small doves which can mix with finches in an aviary.

Base for Mason jar fountain.

Drinking fountain.

heavy soils likely to get soggy, some provision for taking the overflow water away must be made. The use of dripping faucets will increase the total water consumption and cost considerably, but the pronounced advantage of the birds' having ready access all day long to fresh, cool, and clean water is not to be overlooked, especially on hot summer days. To provide excellent bathing facilities a sprinkler system emitting a fine spray may be installed in the aviary and turned on whenever needed. So as not to disturb the birds each time the system is put into operation, it is best to install the control valve outside of the aviary. Most birds much prefer bathing in the spray coming—rainlike—from above to splashing in ordinary pans filled with water. However, owing to their simplicity the latter are much used. Plastic and metal waterpans of varying depth are used for both drinking and bathing. To prevent drowning of birds, the pans should be filled with just enough water to enable the bathers to stand and splash in them. If birds are to be

This closeup of a self-watering set-up shows the constantly fresh water supply dripping from small pipe. The overflow drains into gravel-filled pit below. The cover lifts up for easy accessibility at cleaning time. This set-up was designed by Carl Papp.

The beautiful gold-fronted chloropsis *(Chloropsis aurifrons)* is an extraordinary songbird in spacious, well-planted aviaries, but the brillliant green often blends with the leaves of the plants. However, it is easily tamed and becomes completely confiding even in aviaries.

The black-throated wattle eye *(Platysteira peltata)* from Africa is one of those great rarities which is seldom available even to zoos. The female (on the left) has the black covering nearly all the throat and chest, whereas the male has a rather narrow black band across the chest. All other underparts on the male are white. Wattle eyes are flycatchers and are extremely difficult to maintain in captivity without great quantities of live foods in as wide a variety as possible. Their care is similar to that required by the paradise flycatchers.

kept from using drinking pans for bathing, a wire-net may be spread over the pans' surface. To keep the aviary floor dry, the water dishes may be set on special platforms or in grocery cartons lined with newspaper.

In aviaries in which but few birds are kept, the galvanized pail-like drinking fountains, which hold several gallons of water and thus supply a sufficient amount for several days' use, are very practical, especially since they keep the water reasonably cool. They may be purchased at almost any pet or poultry supply shop and are usually very reasonably priced. If the birdkeeper is unable to give his birds fresh water daily, these fountain drinkers meet his need nicely. To keep the water from freezing in these drinkers in the wintertime, a low-voltage electric light bulb may be kept burning underneath them—a simple but effectual means of insuring a steady supply of water of the right temperature in cold weather.

**Cleaning**

The cleaning of aviaries, etc., is a matter which has to be dealt with regularly. It is useless to allow aviaries to become really dirty and then, only when one feels that they are a disgrace, to set about the task of cleaning. The sensible thing to do is to have regular days for cleaning, and for most fanciers the weekend is the most suitable time. The frequency with which cleaning is carried out will depend, to some extent, upon the owner's spare time, but as a general rule the more frequently cages, aviaries, and such can be cleaned the better. One of the first rules for satisfactory bird-keeping is to provide clean and therefore hygienic accommodations for the birds.

It is a great advantage to have all cleaning equipment in the shelter or bird-room, because there is then no possible excuse for putting off the job which should be done at any particular moment. A long-handled broom with a soft head is extremely useful for sweeping out the shelter floor, and in both bird-rooms and aviaries a brush and dust-pan should be the constant companion of the owner. Attention to detail of this sort may sound trivial, but if one does adopt this careful attitude, it is invariably a hopeful sign for future success in the hobby.

If the trays are left untouched for any length of time, it is probable that the droppings will adhere firmly to them. To remove droppings the use of a scraper is a great help. It is a simple matter to make a useful scraper out of a small piece of wood to the end of which has been fixed a flat piece of metal which does not bend easily.

The rubbish collected in either the bird-room or aviary should immediately be placed in a suitable receptacle so that at intervals it can be taken away to be burned. A small garbage can with a tightly fitting lid is ideal for this purpose. This bin can be kept either inside the shelter or just outside. If you have a bird-room, use a painted bin because it will be more attractive to the eye, even if it is eventually placed unobtrusively somewhere in the corner of the room.

Automatic drinker which fits a wire-front cage.

Catching net.

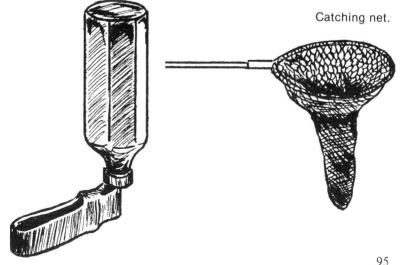

Bullfinch *(Pyrrhula pyrrhula)*. This lovely European bird is very popular with bird lovers. Importation into the U.S. is prohibited, but many bullfinches are admitted annually by government appointees who identify incoming shipments. These birds require small berrylike fruits, buds and insects in addition to a seed mix which contains both canary mix and parrakeet mix. Live food is necessary but should not be confined to mealworms alone.

## Storage Facilities

To store seeds and other miscellaneous supplies safely and conveniently, a portion of the permanent shelter of the aviary or birdhouse, equipped with shelves and cupboards, may well be reserved for this practical purpose. In large metal cans with removable covers seeds may be kept fresh and clean and dustfree for months. If nothing else is available, empty oil drums, which have been thoroughly cleaned, may be used for the purpose. They cost but little and are usually to be had in varying sizes, holding up to a hundred pounds of seed and more.

Various utensils such as catching nets, nest boxes, cages, extra feeders, drinkers, and whatever else is needed in the daily maintenance of the aviary may be conveniently kept in the storage section. In some birdhouses this section occupies a separate room adjoining the permanent shelter. For cleaning and washing dishes and utensils, running water and a wash basin come in very handy in the storage section.

Some birdmen install special shelves in the storage compartment on which they keep cages for single birds which they wish for one reason or another to isolate for a time. Ailing birds requiring special daily treatment are often kept in this way. At any rate, it can readily be seen from the suggestions made above that a separate section for storage, preparation of food, etc., adjoining, or being part of, the permanent shelter of the aviary is very conducive to time and labor saving.

## Hospital Cage Facilities

A so-called hospital cage comes in very handy when temperature control, with provision for extra heat, complete isolation, freedom from drafts and disturbances, and facilities for individual handling and attention are needed.

Heat treatment, especially for egg-bound or otherwise ailing birds, is of paramount importance. Ordinarily, common electric light bulbs, maintaining a temperature up to at least 80 degrees Fahrenheit, but preferably up to 110 degrees, are

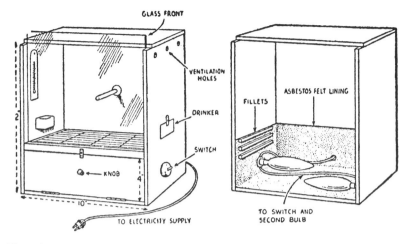

The simple "hospital" at left is for one bird; the diagram at right details the bottom of the interior.

used. The more bulbs are available for this purpose, the better, particularly if provision is made whereby each one may be turned off independently of the others, such provision consisting of a suitable switching arrangement.

Naturally, the size of the hospital cage varies with the average size of the birds to be treated. For accommodating a single parrakeet or canary, a cage twelve inches high, ten inches wide, and six inches deep, is quite suitable. Some fanciers use this size cage, or larger ones, for drying birds after they have been washed.

The figure shows the full cage, made of quarter-inch or three-eighths-inch wood, and provided with a sliding glass front to allow the insertion of the bird and also to retain the heat in the cage. Note the hinged wooden flap at the front, which opens outward and downward to allow access to the light bulbs in the cage. This flap shuts on to the ends of small fillets affixed on the inside of the two sides; it is secured in place by a turn-button fastened to the rail supporting the glass front.

Note that the top of the cage is about one-half inch narrower back to front than is the remainder—in order that the glass front may slide within grooves cut into the inside of both sides. The grooves, about one-eighth inch deep, must be wide enough to make for easy sliding of the glass front.

The glass front rests on the rail fixed across the front of the cage; to make it easy to take hold of it, this front should project about half an inch above the top of the cage.

The fittings for this cage consist of a single perch fixed in the center of the rear, a small thermometer hung on one of the inside walls, and a parrakeet show cage feeder projecting through a hole cut into one side.

The flange at the rear of the feeder rests against the outside of the cage, being held in place by a loosely fixed turn-button. Lastly, there is a show-cage drinker similarly secured through the opposite side of the cage.

Resting on small fillets  fixed across the inside of both sides from front to back  is a light wooden framework containing a portion of an ordinary cage-front or else three-eighths-inch wire netting. This provides a good wire floor through which droppings fall on to a stretcher, preferably white, stretched tightly and sewn to a rectangular frame made from a length of cagewire. This wire is bent into a rectangle of the same size as the inside of the cage and the two ends are soldered together. The stretcher rests also on fillets about one-half inch below the wire floor. It may be readily cleaned by being immersed in boiling water.

Resting on the lowest set of fillets  one-half inch below the stretcher is a sheet of half-inch asbestos, drilled all over with one-half-inch (diameter) holes, one and a half inches apart.

The interior of the cage is lined, up to the level of the top of the fillets, with asbestos felt or similar material used in the making of cooking mats, etc.

The light bulbs are fixed at each end in the base of the cage, there being a switch on one side to control the second light.

The top portion of the cage is best enamelled white inside, and the outside may be finished in any color the fancier chooses.

The lights should be wired so that when the cage is plugged in, one bulb automatically lights, the second and/or additional bulbs being controlled by one or more switches. In this manner, the heat may be regulated, a minimum of 80 degrees being suitable for general purposes. Usually, the two 40-watt bulbs will heat the small cage sufficiently when both are in use. A warming-up period of five minutes is necessary before the cage is ready for treatment; the thermometer should be read frequently to make sure the correct degree of heat is being used.

Once a bird has recovered, reduce the heat gradually, but keep the bird in the cage for half a day or so before returning him to his usual quarters. If need be, the cage may be switched on during the night in perfect safety, provided the wiring is proper.

**Lighting**

Generally speaking birds do not need artificial light, but for the bird-owner it is a great advantage to have his rooms, shelters and aviaries equipped with adequate lighting, otherwise in the winter he will not be able to spend much time, if any, with his birds in the evening. The simplest form of lighting is electric, but there are alternatives. These alternatives may be cheaper, but on the other hand they may be more dangerous. Where electric light is used and the birds are in full light at times when it is dark outside, it is more or less essential to have a dimmer fitted to the circuit. It alarms birds if they are suddenly plunged from full light into darkness. It often scares them so much that if they are not on the perches at the time when the light is put out they immediately fly up to the top of the aviary and may do considerable damage to themselves.

There are a number of dimmers advertised in the fancy press, and these are easy to fit. When they have been set, it is possible to reduce the light gradually so that the birds have an opportunity of settling themselves for the night without any feeling panic.

## Artificial Heat

Few birds require artificial heat in winter, but many of them are, nevertheless, all the better of it. From the point of view of the owner, the ability to heat his shelter or bird-room is extremely valuable. There is no fun at all in working with birds when the temperature is below freezing and one is compelled to wear overcoat and gloves to do what is necessary. There can be no pleasure in the task under such conditions. The simplest form of heating is that provided by electric tubular heaters. They may be rather expensive both to install and to run, but unless the cost is prohibitive, it is certainly more desirable than any other form of heating. The alternative is usually oil, which has its dangers and its almost inevitable smell. If a lamp is left to smoke the birds may come to serious harm, and an oil heater turned up too high has been known to produce a disastrous fire.

Many of the birds which come from tropical countries are quite used to low temperatures at night, and there is no need to keep the temperature of either bird-room or shelter (aviary) above $55^0$ to $60^0$F. with seed-eaters. Some of the more delicate insectivorous or nectar-feeding birds would not survive such low temperatures, but they are not the subject of this book.

Sometimes the bird-owner gets the idea that he should keep his birds in a constant temperature. That idea is entirely wrong and if carried into practice is certainly not good for the birds. In a state of nature they are quite accustomed to very considerable variation between the temperature of day and night, and they are probably fitter and generally hardier because of it. They have their own means of insulation against cold, for with their feathers puffed out they produce excellent insulation against outside cold and thus preserve their body heat.

## Repairs

Minor repairs will have to be undertaken from time to time, and a few simple carpenter's tools should be handy on the spot. A saw, a hammer, a chisel and nails of various lengths, flatheaded, will usually meet the requirements of most jobs that have to be performed as part of the day-to-day routine management.

Some cage wires or netting should also be kept in reserve because in the case of broken cage fronts it is sometimes easier to insert a new wire than to repair an old one, particularly if the old front is rusty. There is a simple reason for this. It is that a good deal of cleaning has to be done before a soldering iron can be used satisfactorily on wire that has become really rusty. This statement, of course, implies that one of the essential pieces of equipment for the bird-keeper is a soldering iron. If he can use an electric soldering iron because he has a source of power close at hand, so much the better, but otherwise he will have to resort to the use of a blow-torch to provide the necessary heat. A soldering iron of some kind is something that must be always available.

# V

# *Practical Aviaries in Use Today*

The purpose of this chapter is not to give you cut and dried rules for building certain aviaries but rather to furnish you with helpful suggestions and suitable illustrations of aviaries which are practical and which you can build yourself, if you wish. Do not, therefore, regard any one of the illustrations given in this chapter as being unchangeable in whole or in part. For, undoubtedly, you wish your particular aviary to suit your particular needs, and usually the needs of no two bird fanciers, or for that matter their tastes, are the same. For this reason you should go over all the illustrations in this chapter with a critical eye and take from each those features which in your opinion fit in best with your needs and desires.

Then, having clearly in mind what you want so far as location, shape, size, and number and kind of birds to be kept are concerned, go ahead and *build your own aviary*. In all probability, it will be different in some respects from any other aviary. That is as it should be, since you want it to meet conditions peculiar to your own personal situation. You may have but little room and you may wish to expend but little money for this part of your hobby. Or, you may have lots of room inside of your house or outside in garden or backyard, and, moreover, you may be ready to build more or less permanently and elaborately, regardless of the monetary cost involved. Whatever your individual situation, there is an aviary to fit your needs, and you are the one to build it.

If you are at all handy with hammer and saw and have the time and the inclination to use them, then you will undoubtedly draw up your own plans and specifications, buy your materials accordingly, and get ready for the busy and enjoyable task of putting up your birds' house. Otherwise, you may simply take your ideas and plans to a reliable local carpenter and have him set up the aviary for you, being thus assured of a more professional job.

## Flight and Closed-In Shelter

A serviceable aviary with attached shelter will appeal to bird fanciers who have but limited space outdoors available for birdkeeping. The simple design is such that the dimensions of house and shelter may readily be shortened or lengthened to suit the builder's space requirements. Thus, if ample space should be available, the aviary can be made not only much longer, but a vestibule providing a very desirable double door may readily be added in front.

A simple garden aviary for canaries and finches.

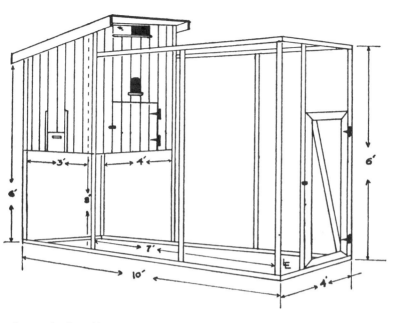

A practical and inexpensive aviary consisting of flight and completely closed-in shelter. The dimensions of this aviary may be easily adjusted to fit the owner's space. Although its size is ample to accommodate numerous birds, the added safeguard of a double door may be added if space permits. If the aviary is to be set on the ground, a cement wall about eighteen inches high should be sunk to foil burrowing animals.

The entire length of this aviary is ten feet, the flight being seven feet long and the shelter three feet long. The flight is six feet high and four feet wide. Height of the shelter is eight feet at the front and six feet at the rear, its width being four feet, and its length or depth three feet.

For the framing of this practical aviary two by twos, or any other suitable size, may be used. If this aviary is set on bare ground, then a cement wall about eighteen inches deep should be sunk in the ground to prevent mice, rats, and other marauders from getting into it. If the aviary is set on a solid, even cement floor, then the wall all around is not needed. If a solid wooden floor is desired, then tongue-and-groove smooth lumber, one by six, is desirable. The wire netting used depends on the size of the birds to be placed in the aviary, preferably half-inch aviary mesh, which comes in four-foot width.

One-inch lumber is used for the roof, which is then covered with a good grade (40 to 60 lbs.) roofing paper. The front of the house is provided with a door for feeding and cleaning. Above it is an entrance and exit hole for the birds. Immediately under the roof is another opening with a sliding glass panel to serve purposes of ventilating and lighting. If the owner prefers, he may use the small sliding side door for feeding and watering his birds. The door to the flight is purposely made small, four feet by two feet, to prevent the birds from escaping. If this aviary is equipped with a vestibule and double doors, then it would be best to make the doors higher for the convenience of the birdkeeper.

A very popular type of aviary consisting of compartmental shelters and flights.

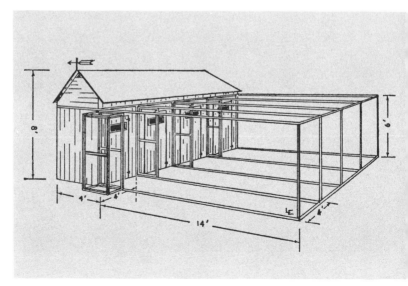

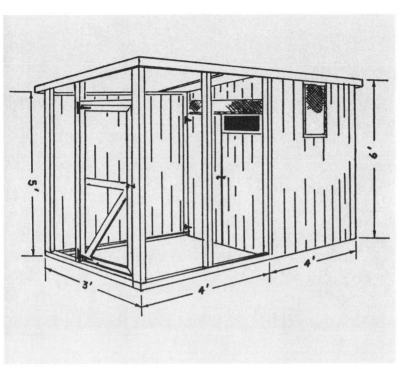

A combination flight and shelter suitable for various types of birds.

In case this aviary is used only during the summer or in regions having suitable weather conditions, its owner may wish to have an open-front house, thus affording his birds inside the house much more air and light. Or he may wish to hinge the entire front of the house so that he can open and close it as becomes necessary.

It is clear that this design is so flexible and simple that it may be suited to almost any birdkeeper's situation. Moreover, its construction requires no expert skill. Anyone handy with hammer and saw can build this bird enclosure in a comparatively short time and at comparatively little expense. Painted white or green, or some other suitable color, this simple but useful structure will not only look attractive, but will give useful service for a good many years.

William Lasky's aviaries have simplicity and trimness in design. The wooden framework and shelters are coated with a finish to enhance the grain of the wood and to blend with a rustic canyon environment. Finches and softbills live amicably in the dense underbrush in these aviaries. Branches and a large clump of weed stalks provide cover and nesting sites for many varieties of birds. Button and harlequin quails especially like the thicket. Running water and growing shrubs add beauty to the central flight at the far end, which contains bulbuls, cardinals, thrushes, tangagers, orioles, and large finches.

## Compartmental Aviary

One aviary illustration accompanying this chapter shows a simply built but practical aviary very popular in the United States. It consists of a permanent house divided into four compartments with flights attached. The compartments are four by four, that is four feet wide and four feet long; their height is seven feet; however, eight feet might be better since birds like to fly up high into the shelter from the flights. The flights are each fourteen feet long and four feet wide, and six feet high. The plan of this layout is of such simple character that the various dimensions may be changed to suit the location and other requirements of the fancier. And there is no limit to the number of compartments and flights which may be added.

The fancier may wish longer and higher flights in order to give his birds more wing exercise. In that case, he should build the house correspondingly higher. If the longer (14 feet) flights are built, additional uprights should be put in on the sides, spaced at forty-eight inch intervals.

To admit more light to the various shelters, the doors may

A beautiful garden birdroom for canaries and Australian finches, such as Lady Goulds.

be made of screen or of celoglass, or similar material. In winter the screen doors may be unhinged and replaced with the regular solid doors to keep the shelters warmer. If it is important that the birds in one compartment do not see or hear those in the adjoining ones, then the partitions in the house may simply be made of wallboard with good insulating qualities; otherwise, hardware cloth may be used between the compartments inside the house or wire netting of suitable mesh size. Note the double-door arrangement at the entrance to the first flight to prevent birds from escaping while the owner enters or leaves the aviary. There are, in addition, doors leading from one flight into the next, as shown in the illustration.

**Combination Flight and Shelter**

In a combination flight and shelter, you have a strongly constructed and very practical aviary, the size of which may be enlarged to suit your special needs and location. It can readily be used for finches, parrakeets, or other birds. Painted a suitable color to harmonize with its immediate surroundings, this birdhouse will be an ornament in any backyard, garden, or other available location. It is so designed as to afford your birds ample light and ample fresh air. With it may be used a concrete floor or else a tight-fitting wooden floor.

The permanent shelter or house is three feet by four feet by six feet high in front, sloping to a height of five feet at the rear. Half-inch or five-eighths inch plywood is used throughout to make a draft-proof, cozy house. The house has a glass window, two feet by one foot, which is covered with wire-mesh on the inside to prevent birds from flying into the glass and so injuring themselves. To the right of the shelter door near the top is a rectangular entrance hole which may be closed by means of a hinged flap. Above this entrance, as well as over the house door, stretches a wire-covered opening to admit light and air into the house. Its height is at least six inches.

The wired-in flight is four feet by three feet by six feet, sloping to five feet. Lumber used for framing consists mainly of two by threes, finished. For the back, which is solidly covered, one-half inch or five-eighths inch plywood may be utilized to advantage, or else finished tongue-and-groove boards, one inch by six inches. Half-inch wire netting may be used to advantage for covering front, one side, and roof. Note that the part of the roof directly above the permanent house door consists of wood covered with roofing paper. It may well be twenty-four inches wide or wider, all depending on the amount of protection from sun or from rain, etc., that is to be given the birds. This portion of the roof, of course, is also designed to prevent strong rains and winds from driving into the flight and from there through the wired panel and entrance hole into the shelter.

The two-foot-wide wire door opens outward. If considered needful, a vestibule with a double door may be built in front of the wire door to prevent the escape of birds. As a whole, this aviary furnishes its occupants good protection without sacrificing facilities for ventilation and light. It may be set on a cement floor to keep rodents from burrowing under and through, or it may be provided with a strong wooden floor made of tongue-and-groove lumber. Painted in pleasing colors, this structure makes a very handy and attractive enclosure for various birds.

**Lean-To Aviary**

As its name suggests, the lean-to birdhouse, consisting of flight and shelter, may readily be placed against house or garden walls. In size it is suited to the height and length of the available wall space. The main point is to have a good, strong slope for the solid roof covering both flight and shelter. Solid roof as well as solid back-wall furnish very good protection—shade in summer and dryness in fall and in winter. If desired, the shelter may be built with one or more glass sides to make it brighter. Of course, such an addition will increase the cost of this very simple but practical (little or big) aviary, which anyone at all handy with saw and hammer can build in a comparatively short time.

Nest boxes may be hung either in the shelter or under the roof of the flight against the wall, where they will be protected from too much sun or wind. Many birds like to roost under such a steeply sloping roof. They may prefer this location to going to roost in the permanent shelter. Of course, the permanent shelter has one or more holes through which the birds may enter and leave. These may be closed at night

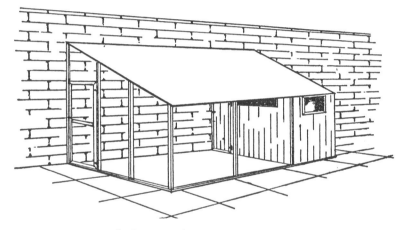

An inexpensive lean-to aviary.

or during inclement weather. In other respects, this lean-to aviary offers excellent opportunity for keeping a mixed collection of birds, as of finches, softbills, and the like. It will also make a very suitable parrakeet enclosure, or, for that matter, is suitable for almost any type of bird or birds.

The dimensions of this lean-to aviary vary with the available space. In other words, this lean-to may be made as long and as high and as wide as its builder desires. It all depends on the number of birds to be kept in it and the amount of space that happens to be available.

## Garden-Type Aviary

If you are at all familiar with types of bird enclosures, you will undoubtedly have seen the garden-type aviary pictured in the figure on page 114, for the reason that it shows one of the most popular kinds of aviaries in use today. The outstanding feature, of course, of this aviary is the rustic roof, which consists of slabs of natural wood of irregular widths with bark. To make the roof waterproof is very essential; therefore this aviary has another roof underneath the top roof, made of tight-fitting wood covered with waterproof paper or other suitable material.

Since the roof affords the bird shelter as well as facilities for nesting, it is purposely made very steep and very spacious. Even though the aviary illustrated here has a flight attached to it, it is often built without such attachment, all depending on the available space and the number of birds to be kept. And according to these two conditions— space available and number of birds to be kept—the size of this aviary may be varied. Being rustic in appearance and simple in layout, this aviary should harmonize especially in height with its surroundings. Thus, if it is to be placed in a garden having rather tall trees, it would be best to build this aviary fairly high, its tallness blending with that of the trees, so to speak.

It should be noted that the roof overhangs the framework by at least a foot in order to prevent rainwater from wetting the underpart. The flight may be extended just as far as the builder wants it to. Some aviaries of this type in actual use have, as a matter of fact, not just one flight attached to the main structure, but flights are attached to several, if not all, sides. Thus, if the bird fancier intends to erect additional flights later on, he should plan to set the roofed-in portion so as to be readily able to accommodate these flights without having to alter the original structure much or to move it to another location.

Over the sides and the top of the flight or flights, climbing

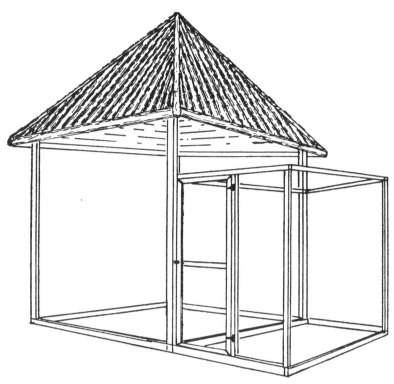
A popular garden-type aviary.

roses or vines may be trained, both for utility—to furnish the birds more shade and some food in the form of live aphids— and for beauty—to enhance the natural appearance of the flight and have it thus blend nicely with its natural surroundings.

To protect the occupants of the roofed-in portion from fright caused by strangers or animals approaching suddenly, one or more of its sides or walls may be glassed in or boarded in. The glassed-in walls would be covered with wire netting or hardware cloth on the inside for the birds' protection. Otherwise, ordinary tongue-and-groove lumber or wallboard may be used to wall in one or more sides, and these may be painted a suitable color to blend with the surroundings.

Kenneth Wyatt's aviary houses Australian finches and such Australian parrakeets as redrumps, elegants and Bourkes. The birds are compatible and are prolific breeders. Mr. Wyatt has broken several of the experts' rules and has had phenomenal success with his birds.

115

Such walling-in of sides also provides additional protection to the birds from wind and weather.

Ordinarily, this type of aviary is best entered from the flight, which may be equipped with a double door. By entering from the flight, the fancier will compel any birds being in it at the time to seek the haven of the roofed-in shelter and so to get quickly out of his way. Owing to this condition, a double door may not be necessary.

This rustic aviary derives part of its popularity from its simple construction and practical usefulness. It is meant mainly for summer occupancy in regions with cold winters, but in regions with milder climates the birds may be left in it the year around. It is suitable for practically all kinds of flying birds, especially if kept for more or less ornamental and hobby purposes and not mainly for breeding. For, if the nestboxes be hung under the steep roof, control of nesting activities by the fancier is thereby made a little awkward, though not necessarily so. Some fanciers prefer not to control nesting activities at all—not to disturb their birds during breeding season.

As has been mentioned several times before, it is well to creosote all lumber used in the construction of any aviary in order to repel mites and the like. Such precautions taken at the right time will save the fancier much extra grief and work later on.

It should be added also that while in a garden setting this particular style of aviary would probably look its most natural if provided with a rustic-looking roof, any other type of roof may be used and serve the particular purpose of the fancier just as well, or even better. The illustrations given in this section of the book are meant to be helpful and suggestive—not to lay down hard and fast rules for building aviaries. In other words, the prospective builder of an aviary will modify the aviary illustrated to fit his location, his birds, and his other needs and ideas, and will thus suit himself.

## Inside Aviaries

Many men and women fond of birds and desirous of keeping some, but living in houses having no gardens or other suitable outdoor locations for aviaries, have to resort to indoor bird keeping. Moreover, some cities have in recent years passed so-called health ordinances forbidding all bird-keeping outdoors, particularly so in more or less congested

A conservatory aviary is an excellent and beautiful environment for those softbills which do not destroy foliage. Humidity must be kept low for most softbills. Those which require especially high humidity are only for the experts.

towns and cities, where outdoor aviaries would have to be set rather close to neighboring properties.

Quite often such men and women have some space to spare inside—it may be a spare, unused room or part of one, or part of a garage, attic, porch, or cellar. So long as this inside birdroom to-be is reasonably light, draft-proof, dry, and can be kept fairly warm in winter, it will keep birds in good health. Certainly, whatever desirable characteristics possessed by an outdoor aviary this inside bird-enclosure lacks, it most assuredly has the great advantage of accessibility. The fancier has his birds right close by—does not usually have to go out in rainy or wintry weather to look after his feathered friends since they are very conveniently with him in his house. Moreover, no neighbor is likely to complain about the fancier's hobby, it being none of his business what the latter keeps *inside* his dwelling or garage, or other outhouse. Finally, being usually already built, the inside birdroom is largely ready for the occupancy of the birds. Their owner certainly does not have to start from scratch, so to speak. All he usually has to do is to suit the available space to the needs of whatever kinds and number of birds he intends to stock it with. In other words, his problem is not so much one of building a new structure as one of equipping to the best advantage one already built.

**Attic Aviary**

A very reasonably-priced aviary may be constructed in the attic where the aviary wire is nailed to rafters, studding, and the like. Both the attic floor and the flight floor should be covered with some good waterproof, cleanable material. Sheet aluminum would be good for the flight floor, and also for the roof of the flight.

The inside compartment may vary in shape as well as in size to fit the amount of space available. The outside flight would be approximately three feet by three feet by three feet. The roof, boarded up and covered, slopes slightly away from the house.

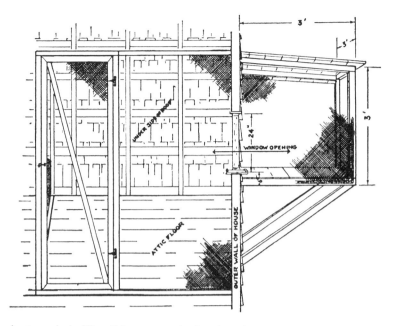

In crowded cities this economical attic aviary will provide adequate housing. Note that an outdoor flight is suspended from the outer wall of the dwelling. This system is best for accommodating a limited number of birds.

The floor of the flight should be only a few inches—five or six—below the window sill. This arrangement will allow for reaching out through the window when one cleans or does other chores. The window should be from eighteen to twenty-four inches square, and it may have a hinged flap-door. For good circulation of air, the attic should have other air-vents or windows.

This same sort of plan may be used for a cellar aviary, provided that the foundation walls are sufficiently high (house-floor far enough above the ground level) to permit an outside flight. In this case, the flight would rest upon the ground outside.

If these conditions do not exist, the cellar aviary would be entirely inside, and the need for good air-vents and/or screened windows, as well as suitable lighting, would be obvious.

Needless to say, there are many aviculturists who do an excellent job of keeping and raising birds in limited space—in the corner of a garage or other outhouse, in a snug attic with plenty of light and air, even in a cellar equipped with suitable lighting and ventilating facilities. Whatever the location, the requirements of the birds' health—plenty of fresh air; sunlight, if possible; freedom from wet and damp cold; sufficient room within which to exercise their wings; and no crowding must be met. These essentials should prevail and must be provided whether the birds are kept outside or inside. Certainly, birds will not thrive in foul air or in artificial light, no matter how well fed they may be. In locating a desirable place for an indoor aviary, therefore, the fancier should consider that place which is likely to give the birds sufficient fresh air and sufficient sunlight. The other essentials—freedom from draft, from wet or damp cold, from crowding, etc. —he can readily provide in almost any location that has plenty of light and plenty of good fresh air. Since birds prefer the morning sunlight to the afternoon sunlight, a location for the inside birdroom should preferably face east or southeast. If the inside birdroom gets the benefit of sunlight for only part of the day, then artificial light must be provided for the rest of the day.

Fresh air in inside birdrooms is usually provided either by windows or by special ventilators having been installed for the purpose. When the windows are opened, the frames reveal their having been covered with wire netting or other suitable material. If heat has to be supplied at any time, hot-water pipes or electric appliances are usually found to be the most suitable, even though almost any kind of heat is suitable provided it does not come from an open gas flame in the birdroom and is not too dry or at all smelly. Most inside birdrooms, being well protected by solid walls from outside temperatures, require no heating in the winter. Being

A suggestion for a simple indoor enclosure.

The interior of Mr. Papp's planted aviary offers and abundance of nesting sites of every description. One style of nest preferred by some finches is this bank of dried grasses held in place by a grate. This grass apartment can house many nests.

thoroughly dry and draft-proof, all except probably delicate tropical birds would thrive in such rooms, that is, without extra heat being furnished.

If a spare room in the house is to be converted into an inside aviary, care must be taken to protect floor and walls from being spoiled for future use. Thus, it is best to cover the walls with a thin layer of wallboard or insulating material and the floor with a special layer of tar paper, linoleum or other more or less waterproof material. On top of this special layer may be placed a layer of sand to the depth of several inches, or simply, and most inexpensively, a layer of paper, newspaper or somewhat heavier but still absorptive paper, which can be readily replaced. If there is any likelihood of mice entering the inside birdroom, then the floor and the sides all around at least six inches high are best covered with some sheet or other metal, for there can be no successful birdkeeping if mice bother the birds at night or in the day. And while there may be no mice when at first the inside birdkeeping has been started, the presence of seeds will attract them to any inside aviary, and they will go to considerable pains to seek and to make entrances into this aviary. It is therefore common sense to keep them out right from the first by making the room mouseproof, as suggested above.

The matter of equipping an inside birdroom is very much the same as that of "furnishing" an outside aviary. Nest boxes are hung along the walls at suitable distances. Perches are fastened as far apart as possible to compel the birds to fly, and in such places where they will not interfere too much with the fancier's having ready accessibility to various parts of the room. Drinkers and feeders are placed where most accessible for the birds as well as for their keeper. Suitable receptacles are placed under both drinkers and feeders to catch overflows of water or seed and thus prevent this overflow from getting onto the floor of the room, necessitating a lot of cleaning.

If the owner of an inside birdroom wants it to appear

natural, he can fasten branches with or without leaves along the walls of the room and place living plants in pots in various parts of the room. When soiled or spoiled, the living plants will of course have to be renewed. If canaries and other birds likely to eat the leaves off such plants are to be kept, then live plants cannot be used in the inside birdroom—at least not for atmosphere or decoration. But keepers of softbills can decorate the inside birdroom very naturally and fittingly, since their birds will not pull the leaves off plants and eat them. Incidentally, large, live plants placed in such birdrooms will certainly improve the air in them. Their leaves may be sprayed periodically to keep them clean and freshlooking. Some inside birdrooms are equipped with miniature fountains, the fine spray of which prevents the air from getting too dry, thus keeping the birds' plumage glossy and buoyant. Ingenious birdmen will find all sorts of means to individualize the inside equipment of their birdrooms without sacrificing naturalness for the birds' surroundings. After all is said and done, birds are nature's very own creatures and should be kept in surroundings looking as natural as possible. To clutter up a birdroom with all kinds of artificial bird "furniture" is unwise. The simpler and the more practical the equipment of an inside birdroom, the better it is likely to suit its occupants. By no means should the room be crowded with equipment, thus preventing its owner from seeing his birds quickly and at any time. This does not mean, of course, that he should not provide his birds with some suitable places in which to hide, but such places should be few in number and strategically located in the room. Needless to say, birds kept in rooms become very tame in a reasonably short time and will therefore not want to hide from their owner.

The part of any inside birdroom likely to be soiled most by its occupants undoubtedly is the walls. For this reason, the fancier should make provision for being able to clean them readily—for washing them repeatedly and without too much trouble. Whatever material, therefore, he decides to use on the walls of the inside birdroom, it should "take" a periodic washing readily.

The feeding station for this aviary designed by Carl Papp is in the enclosed bird room so that birds show no hesitation about entering and so that feeding arrangements do not mar natural appearance of the outside flight. *Pyracantha* berries are greatly enjoyed by many birds.

# VI

# Brief Descriptions of Successful Fanciers' Aviaries

Undoubtedly, many a bird fancier about to build an aviary would very much like to get first-hand and thoroughly practical information from an old hand in the hobby, talk with him or her personally and so get direct answers to questions and many little tips of a helpful character. Unfortunately, few fanciers are so situated that they can call on numerous fellow fanciers having the sort of information they need.

In order to help solve this personal problem, it has been deemed expedient in this, the final chapter of this book to furnish the reader with successful bird fanciers' comments on their own aviaries and birdkeeping facilities. These comments pertain to the most interesting and helpful aspects mentioned by these men and women, who have been generous in furnishing these helpful data. In most cases the comments represent excerpts from statements made by these fanciers, since there is not space sufficient here to print their entire statements.

Commenting on a small aviary for a beginner, an old-time fancier, very successful in birdkeeping, writes in part:

"The first thing to do is to measure your ground to see what size aviary you can erect—what size flight and what size shelter you can have. Then take a piece of paper and draw up your ground-plan, then the front and end views of the structure. You or your carpenter can work better if you have a plan, however simple, on paper.

"I built the covered part of my aviary first; it measures six feet from back to front, is four feet wide and seven feet high at the rear, and six feet at the front. In front I left a space for a window, which is about two feet by one foot, six inches. I built this shelter with three by three posts and three by one and one-half inch crossbars and covered the house with a roof of three-quarter inch tongue-and-groove sheeting. This house I set on a cement floor several inches thick and sunk in cement walls all around to a depth of sixteen inches to keep water and vermin from getting in. At the side of this house I left space for a door leading into the flight, also a small opening for the birds to get in and out during the winter, when I keep the door shut.

This indoor aviary for finches has a hamper for dried grasses used for building nests such as the carefully constructed nest in the upper right hand corner of the photo.

"Next I made the flight—twelve feet long, six feet deep, six feet high in front, and seven feet high in the rear. I used three by three posts, with cross pieces and rafters being three by one and one-half inches. The roof I covered four feet over the flight up to the middle post, thus making a good outside shelter on wet and stormy days. I also extended the roof along the back of the open part, but only fourteen inches deep to protect nest boxes, feeders, etc. The back was made of three-quarter inch tongue-and-groove lumber. All roofs were covered with a sixty-pound roofing paper.

"The floor of the flight was made also of cement, sloping toward the front to allow for run-off of water and to make hosing and cleaning easier. I covered the flight with half-inch netting, which in turn I varnished thoroughly to keep it from rusting in our wet climate. After five years' use, the netting is as good as ever.

"Painting was the next item of procedure. At first I was doubtful about painting, having heard of birds nibbling the lead paint and dying. However, I risked painting, letting it dry thoroughly, and no harm came to any of my birds from this feature. The painting looks clean and is easily renewed each year. Inside the shelter I used white, and outside, green paint.

"I feed my birds from so-called self-feeders which hold three pounds of seed. For drinking I use white enamel dishes, which do not seem to show the green scum produced in pottery containers. In a big, wood tray I place sand and broken-up old mortar, which the birds seem to love judging from the fact that they are constantly picking in it and at it. The tray is protected from rain to keep it dry. In this small aviary I started with four pairs of parrakeets, which multiplied the first season so much that I disposed of dozens of youngsters at the end of it. In other words, the birds found their home suitable for their needs, and that is all that counts."

Another fancier who moved into a new home had to erect

new aviaries and explains their construction in part as follows:

"While I built my old aviaries myself, my new ones had to be erected in three months time and so I had to hire several men for the heavy work and a carpenter part-time, with me doing the supervising of the whole job.

"At the beginning I got a sound wooden shed, built of four by three-inch quartering and feather-edge boards. Its roof was in bad condition, and was 20 feet long by 18 feet wide, being 15 feet high. The ground available was a strip 54 feet long and 20 feet wide. By setting the shed in the middle of this space, I was able to wire in two flights 18 by 20 feet at each side of the shed. The two gable ends of the shed were put up first, ridge board and rafters following. A large skylight was put in to each slope of the roof, which was then boarded and covered with a heavy-weight roofing paper.

"The sides of the shelter were not boarded but glazed, the glass being stippled with white paint, which obviates the necessity of wire-netting to protect the birds from injury. The shed was divided by half-inch mesh-wire partitions into four compartments, each ten by nine feet. Each compartment opens by means of a glazed door into an outside flight, ten by eighteen feet. In cold weather the doors are kept shut and the birds are allowed to fly in and out of the shelter through a small trapdoor placed above each door and worked by cord and pulley.

"The floor of the shelter is cemented, and each compartment is provided with a three-foot high metal post on which the feeding tray is set, thus preventing mice from climbing up and getting at the feed. All doors leading from one compartment to the next are equipped with a special spring, thus preventing birds from getting accidentally into the wrong compartment. The outside flights, 18 by 10, are eight feet high and covered with three-eighths inch mesh-netting, which, however, has not kept out mice despite the cement foundation sunk into the ground all around the aviaries.

This is a series of typical outdoor aviaries seen in zoos and bird parks.

"I have found that all birds prefer to roost high, and they can readily be induced to roost in the shelter, provided it is higher than the flights, thus being safe from storms, rain and cold, and cats. While referring to cats, I must explain that I have installed rectangular wire brackets to project two feet all around the tops of the flights, on which is stretched one-inch wire netting, this scheme making the top of the aviary absolutely inaccessible to cats.

"Each of the flights is provided with a cement-made bath, fitted with a plug and an overflow. There is a cement path running the length of each flight, which I find easy to keep clean, and on which I sprinkle tidbits of seed, etc.; gravel paths, on the other hand, are likely to become foul soon.

"All doors opening from the garden into the flights push inward and are eighteen inches lower than the flights themselves, thus greatly reducing the chances of a bird escaping when I enter the aviaries.

"In these aviaries I keep finches, buntings, sugar birds, thrushes, and quail, keeping each variety separately, if at all possible. The birds have been doing nicely in their new homes, which I consider quite satisfactory for their needs and my purposes."

An enthusiastic breeder of canaries on the Pacific coast has this to say regarding proper housing:

"An aviary for canaries should be built to take care of the number of birds one intends to keep. Out here we use a building with lots of windows for plenty of sunlight, and, of course, one that is absolutely free from drafts. It is well to have a flight adjoining this shelter, with wire on all sides. The most suitable wire I find is one-half inch hardware cloth. If the aviary is on a breezy corner, it may be well to cover one or more sides of the flights with plastic cloth.

"The size of the aviary depends entirely on the number of birds kept, and they will always do better if they are not

This divided aviary was constructed by an aviculturist in an urban area.

crowded. A good size for approximately 35 birds is an aviary that is eight feet high, four feet wide, and eight feet long, with a flight of about the same size attached. The shelter should be higher than the flight since when being chased into the shelter at night, the birds tend to fly high and will enter the shelter much faster if it is high—higher than the flight.

"The floor of the shelter is covered with newspapers which are changed weekly. All seeds in their containers are placed in grocery cartons, which catch those that the birds scatter and thus keep the floor fairly clean. A shallow water dish, eight or nine inches in diameter, is also placed in a carton heavily padded with newspapers, which method keeps the floor of the shelter dry and thus prevents any seed on the floor from souring.

"When canaries begin to roost at night, they quarrel for the best places. To stop this nightly trouble we use individual roosts for our birds, which swing from overhead on hooks and eyes. The roosts are cut from a one by four with a jigsaw and then a dowel is screwed to the bottom of it.

"To avoid having mites, be sure to saturate all lumber used for the aviary and flights with creosote, excepting, of course, the perches and places where the birds are likely to stand or sit. Mice you can eliminate by using a cement floor in your aviary and then building a smooth wall two or three feet high all around your aviary and flights. Mice will squeeze through half-inch wire, but they cannot climb or jump over a smooth surface twenty-four or more inches high. Another protection would be simply to use one-quarter inch netting."

A Midwestern bird enthusiast reports as follows on his way of housing his birds:

"For convenience and also because of the bad weather we frequently get here in winter, I keep my birds inside—in one large birdroom, which adjoins my bedroom, there being a large  double door between, so I can look after my birds any time and do not have to go outside in all kinds of weather. Across the south side are four large windows to let in plenty of light and sunshine. In addition I have two large flights—one across the west end of the room, in which I winter my breeding hens. During the breeding season, I remove the large front and put in shelves for the breeding cages. I leave the cages there till fall, then remove and put on the wirefronts. All this makes an ideal arrangement, since the birds get sun all morning and plenty of light.

"Across the east end of the same room is another flight, where I winter the breeding males, and where they get sun all afternoon. On the north side of the room is a bench and cabinet where I keep record books, bands, and miscellaneous supplies. Since I have no extra space, I have to utilize every inch of space in this one birdroom.

"Most breeders in the Middle West do not use outside aviaries owing to the inclement weather we get in this section of the country."

A breeder of canaries and other seedeaters in New York State brings interesting news concerning his aviary:

"My aviary is joined to the rear of my garage, and I have an outdoor flight in which I keep the female canaries, etc. in the summer. It is 3 x 6 x 5, made in sections so that it may be taken down in winter, and set on a concrete base. I use window-screen to keep out mosquitoes, flies, and the like.

"The size of the aviary is 12 x 6 x 6. My house stands on a hill, but the garage and the aviary are below the ground about 18 inches, to which depth I dug the soil out and laid a concrete floor, above which I laid two rows of blocks, with the result that the aviary stands four inches above the ground. To keep the moisture out I put a good, thick coat of tar on the floor of the aviary.

"I used 2 x 4's for framing and wood shingles to match the garage. The roof of the aviary has a 6 inch pitch and is equipped with 2 sky lights 2 by 2 feet square, which admit plenty of light and sun. Also in the roof I have an automatic ventil-

African grey parrots are popular aviary and pet birds because of their talking ability.

ator, 8 inches square, which closes automatically when a strong wind begins to blow. I covered the walls with a fiberboard which I gave a heavy coat of shellac to seal all small holes; then I painted it a light blue, which seems to show the birds off to better advantage. The window to the south, 15 by 30 inches, is screened; on hot days it is opened by means of a crank. I use fluorescent lights in the ceiling, 14-watt light blue day-light bulbs. The sky lights are covered on the inside with celoglass to shade the bright sun in the day.

"For heat I use a thermostatically controlled heater, which I keep at about 70 degrees throughout the winter months."

The following report is from an aviculturist who lives in a damp region of the country:

"My first aviary was built three years ago against the glassed-in west end of a conservatory, which thus protects it from the east and slightly warms that side of it. It is in the form of a cube seven feet to the eave of the roof, a gabled one, sloping north and south. The lower half of the south side of the roof is made of glass to let more sunshine in; the upper half and the whole north side of the roof consist of boards covered with heavy roofing paper.

"The front of the aviary to the south is the only open side. It is covered with smallest available mesh-netting, about two feet of the west side made of glass, the rest of this side and the whole of the back made of boards covered with roofing

Breeding of the turquoisine grass parakeet in aviaries helped to save this bird from extinction.

paper. The floor is concrete, laid on a brick foundation, and raised about eight inches above the ground. In the wintertime a wooden blind is drawn over the wire front of the aviary at night.

"With varying success I have kept for the last three years in this aviary Parsons finches, diamond sparrows, silverbills, avadavats, goldfinches, and many other kinds. In this cold and damp region, my birds have withstood 35 to 40 degrees of frost last winter, even though some of the avadavats suffered from this cold. In building an aviary, I am convinced that plenty of sunshine is the most essential point so far as a suitable location is concerned."

A fancier in Minnesota presents the following informative description of her birdroom:

"Since we are controlled by city ordinances prohibiting the keeping of birds outdoors inside the city limits, I house my birds in the basement. The part of it I use is L-shaped— 24 feet long and 22 feet wide. I have three flights on the west wall, each being 9 feet deep, 5 feet wide, and 6½ feet high. One-quarter inch mesh-wire is used. Two large feeders hang suspended by wire, each holding ten pounds of seed or grit. Near the door is a feeding table with grit, supplement, greens, and drinking dishes.

"Our nest boxes (for parrakeets) are 9 inches by 9 inches by 9 inches, have a concave bottom block that slides out for easy cleaning, and open on a hinge at the back."

An old-time fancier residing in a region often subject to cold weather describes her aviary concretely as follows:

"My aviary housing small finches and other similar birds stands in a sunny orchard. Set against a high brick wall, it faces due south.

"The house or shelter is composed of two thicknesses of wood with felt between; and the span roof is made of corrugated iron lined with wood, the whole having been varnished inside except the back wall, which is whitewashed. The dimensions are 16 feet long by 9½ feet wide and 13½ feet high at the highest point of the roof. The front of the aviary is wired to within two feet of the ground, and along the entire length ten glass-panelled movable shutters are fastened. In summer the shutters are removed, but in cold weather they are all kept up, forming a large window, 16 feet long by 5½ feet high. All shutters can be installed or removed in a few moments.

"Added on to each front end of the aviary is a wooden porch with double doors, the outer made with glass panels, the inner with wire netting. Inside each porch is a shelf for seed containers and supplies, located over the door. Climbing roses run over the house, greatly improving its appearance, since it is a very plain structure. There is a window at each end of the aviary and two sky lights in the roof, which may be readily opened.

"Inside, the house is divided by wire partitions, making two compartments. A constantly running water supply is available for the birds in stone basins so shaped that the birds can bathe at any depth they wish. The waste water is carried away by a one inch pipe.

"At first I used a glass floor in the aviary, which, however, I found hard to keep clean. Then I substituted gray tiles, which are sprinkled with fresh sand once a week and which I find more satisfactory. At various places in the aviary I have fixed wooden blocks with holes in them, into which tree branches of various thicknesses are screwed to serve as perches for the birds. Fastened in this wise, the perches are not likely to fall down or get loose easily.

"Once a year the whole aviary is thoroughly cleaned from top to bottom, all woodwork being given a thorough scrubbing with soap and water, and the back wall being whitewashed. I use electric heat in the aviary on cold winter days and nights, and my birds keep in good health. I have kept mostly finches of various kinds and some smaller foreign doves, all of which seem to get along very nicely in the enclosures I have briefly described above."

Each pen in this double row of parakeet breeding pens is 7' high, 2'8" wide and 8' long.

**Opposite:**
These are aviaries constructed for
lovebirds.

A Western Canadian bird fancier uses aviaries 30 feet long, 7 feet high, and 14 feet wide. They are set on a cement slab, two by three's for framing, shiplap on the outside, tar paper and siding and Duroid roof, insulated throughout, lined with plywood on the inside, the outside partitions being two by two's.

On the inside back wall are two tiers of breeding compartments, ten in each row, or twenty altogether, each compartment having a 12 x 20-inch window which is rabbeted to prevent drafts and which can be opened at any time. Each compartment front is framed out of two-by-two's and is rabbeted to fit in each compartment and buttoned on, being completely removable for cleaning.

Each compartment is divided with half-inch mesh and equipped with a door 13" x 20" with a one by two-inch strip on which to hang the feeding tray. Each tray is 10 inches wide and shaped like a half circle, with a guard-edge of three-quarters of an inch to prevent food from being strewn over the floor. Seed hoppers and water fountains are in each compartment. A one-by one-quarter inch strip is fastened on the heater to the left side of each door with a screw to hang nest boxes, which in this way face a window and get full benefit of light.

Under the lower compartments the full length of the aviary there is a one-foot storage space. The passageway is two feet, six inches, with a door equipped with ventilator at the bottom at one end, and a window at the other end with a ventilator which can be opened or closed. This lower vent brings in the fresh air, while the stale air rises and escapes through the top ventilator.

Breeding pens in the front are three by three by seven, framed outside with two by two's, with a door eighteen inches wide in each pen, two by five, with feeding trays similar to the ones on the back compartments. Bob holes are six feet off the ground, three inches wide, and one-half inch round, lined with galvanized iron, and two by three in between the walls, with a two by two landing inside and out, and equipped with shutters that can be closed.

Outside flights are three feet, six inches by three feet, and seven feet high, framed out of two by three's, with half-inch wire netting between them, double wire on top, there being a three-inch space over the flights as a safeguard against cats. Duroid roof with a ten-inch overhang is used for rain protection.

The two center pens are used for young birds, after the partition has been removed to afford double space. This pen is equipped with a bicycle wheel rim on the wall between the two windows which have protruding perches riveted on. On this wheel the youngsters get much exercise. Each pen is equipped with a door leading into the cat walk, which is two feet wide, six feet high, with a pitch to meet the outside open flights. The doors are two feet wide and five feet high.

All woodwork in this aviary is painted with white enamel, the wire with black enamel; neither enamel contains lead. Lighting fixtures are fluorescent. The aviaries are unheated, the full insulation keeping the aviary at or just above the body warmth of the birds. The breeding pens with attached flights are used for control breeding during the season; later they house at least twenty birds each, giving them excellent opportunity to fly all winter through. The birds are so housed that rain may fall on them in the flights, which is very beneficial for them since all members of the parrot family enjoy an occasional wetting of this sort.

A successful Texas parrakeet fancier uses an aviary seventy-eight feet long divided into fifteen separate pens, each having flight and breeding space. Each door connecting breeding compartment with flight has a door equipped with a small, sliding "speak-easy" type panel, which is opened in cold weather when the door itself is closed. The lower panel is reserved for button quail, kept largely to eat up the scattered seeds, and for young budgies venturing from breeding pens into flights.

These budgerigar aviaries allow the birds to have access to the inside areas as well as outdoor flights.

Each unit houses fifty. pairs of parrakeets. Each flight has an ornamental drinking fountain with its own water spigot, the water being piped from a deep well on an adjoining hill.

A hallway lined with sliding, screened-in windows runs the entire length of the building. Midway is a door to reduce the space involved when capturing escapees from the breeding rooms, the doors of which open onto the hallway. The latter has a cement floor, electric lights, and a sink at one end used for cleaning purposes.

The aviary entrance leads into a commodious workshop equipped with power tools for building nest boxes and equipment. This shop has a cement floor and is used also for seed storage. Leading from this room are the hallway and the doors to the fifteen pens. The interior of the aviary is painted white and the exterior silver to deflect the hot rays of the boiling Texas sun. A high grade composition roof tops the aviary, the floors being concrete for the breeding rooms and

142

The aviary for these Queen of Bavaria conures is very large in order to allow the birds ample space in which to exercise.

gravel for the flights.

A noted English fancier, whose aviary is a pleasure to visit, uses a birdroom with batteries of six cages fitted into angle-iron frames, two cages per tier. The cages, measuring 30" x 12" x 12", are of galvanized sheet, stove-enamelled white throughout. All feeding, watering, etc., is done at the rear of the cages, the fronts of the feed hoppers being flush with the interior rear wall so that nothing can be fouled. In front of the hoppers is a suitably placed perch, and below is a strip of inclined metal to shoot the husks on to the wire-mesh floor of the cage.

It should be noted that the hoppers hold feed sufficient for twenty-one days and that the water supply is provided automatically—always fresh.

The floor of each cage is made of three-quarter-inch wire-mesh fixed in a suitable frame so that all droppings, seed husks, etc., fall through onto an inclined metal ramp, from which this waste-matter drops into a large trough running with a slight slope the whole length of the batteries, from which it can be swept rapidly into a bin for removal from the birdroom. Every fitting in this aviary can be dismantled in a few seconds. Not only is the entire birdroom hygienic, but some sixty cages can be thoroughly cleaned in one hour!

A large, neatly constructed nest box is hung at the rear of each cage, with the entrance hole facing the light. Made of stove-enamelled galvanized sheet, this nest box has a removable wooden interior.

The building used by this ingenious fancier is a thick-walled outhouse, some 48 feet long, 18 feet wide, and 15 feet high, with a considerable length of Perspex roof lighting on the west side and several large windows on the opposite side. His all-metal breeding compartments arranged in two rows total sixty, with additional units at the two ends of the building. Facing the west is a range of large flights.

One of the most striking features of the equipment is the artificial lighting for winter use. It consists of rows of special daylight electric bulbs fitted beneath long reflectors—giving light at the fronts of the cages—and a row of ordinary bulbs midway over the backs of the compartments facilitates cleaning-out operations during the short days. The daylight bulbs are controlled by a time-switch.

Artificial lighting with daylight bulbs permits breeding all year. After a pair has raised its nest, the young are put in the nursery flight, and the parents are put in segregated flights. Breeding cages are then ready for the next pair.

The room is perfectly ventilated and the birds are never troubled with mites or parasites of any sort, nor are they ever afflicted with French molt. Breeding conditions and results have been satisfactory each year.

Meticulous records of all vital statistics, and other data, are kept on each bird. Every bird is banded.

An Idaho doctor writes of the aviary he and his father-in-law built in their spare time:

"I have at last finished my new birdhouse. For years my constantly growing collection of birds has presented a housing problem in winter. When a sudden cold spell froze the feet on some lovebirds I decided that I would have to be more considerate of my birds and provide some heat for them since I couldn't bring them all in the house.

"I had been reading about aviaries and bird housing and gradually formulating a plan for a new house. I would like to point out some of the features incorporated in it that I think are advantageous and might be of interest to others who may be contemplating such an adventure.

"The dimensions decided upon were thirty feet long by twelve feet wide inside. It was to have a four foot center aisle with cages on either side, each cage being three feet wide. We began by digging a foundation footing; then, with the footing laid as near level as possible, forms only for the outside were made. The center area was then leveled and filled in with rock to within three to four inches of the top of the forms, leaving space inside the forms for a good foundation.

Cockatiels were kept in the same aviary as this pair of Bourke's parakeets (or parrots).

The whole was poured at one time as a level slab. My father-in-law, who is an expert in concrete work, put on a wonderfully smooth finish. An inclined ramp leads from the door to the ground level so that a wheelbarrow may be used when needed.

"The framework of two by fours was put up. The studding was placed eighteen inches apart so that solid nailing for the three foot cage partitions could be made. The inside walls were lined with pressed wood wallboard in four by six foot sections. The outside walls of lumber siding were then put up and the space between walls filled with shavings for insulation as the work progressed.

"There are no window openings in the walls on either

Zebra finches are one of the most popular aviary birds. These birds are fine songsters, are easy to care for and are easy to breed. Zebras also offer a breeder the opportunity to experiment with variations from the normal gray color shown here.

side, as it was planned to have all light enter from the center part of the roof, thus making window cleaning and protection from breaking by the birds unnecessary. Therefore, it was necessary to very accurately space the rafters eighteen inches apart as the glass panes would fit. The roof with a two foot overhang was then finished with solid sheeting, tar paper, and asphalt shingles up to where the window openings come near the peak of the roof. The window panes of double thickness glass were seventeen by twenty-six inches.

"To lay the glass the two by four ends left from the rafters were ripped with a power saw into two by twos; then strips about three-eighths by five-eighths inches were ripped out on each side of the upper edge. These were nailed onto the rafters making a frame for the glass to lie on. A one by eight was placed on either side of the peak with a piece ripped out on the lower underside so that the glass panes could be shoved about an inch under to keep out rain. To lay the panes, caulking compound was applied with a caulking gun. This can be done easily and rapidly and makes a very effective seal. The lower end of the panes overlapped the shingles two inches, with a line of caulking compound to seal it and a shingle nail to keep the glass from sliding down until the caulking compound dried.

"With the roof finished, I then had an electrician install a wall type electric heater with a thermostat in the center of the end wall and three two tube fluorescent lights connected with the timer in my chicken house to automatically lengthen the day. Now during the winter I could work at my leisure to finish the interior.

"A three foot wide space to the sink of the door was reserved for a sort of kitchen, and a sink was placed against the wall with water piped in. The only wall window is here, giving side light for washing procedures.

"It was thought to be impractical and unnecessary to have the cages from floor to ceiling, so two by four framework with the floor joists three feet apart were erected and tongue and groove flooring was laid, making a platform four feet wide to be the floor for the cages. Now with this to stand on the ceiling was covered with hard wallboard also used for the walls. The space between the rafters was filled with shavings, as were the walls. The open ends were closed with left-over pieces of wallboard cut to fit tightly.

"Provision was made for wire bottoms for the cages by nailing two by fours on edge at three foot intervals to mark the cage partitions, thus leaving a four inch space for cleaning under the wire floor. The cages were made three and a half feet deep, leaving a six inch shelf in front of the cages which I find is very convenient to set things on while opening the doors. The framing now was of two by twos. A door was made for each cage which is large enough for one to climb through to paint the inside. The cages are separated by three-ply plywood for privacy and avoidance of drafts. To make use of the space below the upper deck on the south side this space was divided into three foot sections for ground birds such as quail. Just how satisfactory this will be I don't know, but a late-hatched silver pheasant seems very satisfied and spends much more time inside than in the run outside.

"The north side space has a section of drawers and cupboards salvaged from a house I tore down. Also mouse-proof feed bins, a large bin for sawdust and one for sand, are available.

"This gives nineteen upper compartments and nine lower ones for birds. The south side is covered with one third inch hardware cloth for small birds and the north with one by two welded wire except for two cages with two by four wire. In these I hope to have parrots, thus the heavy wire. Each cage has a long perch made of a vertical board with two cross pieces at right angles.

"A word about making doors may be useful as this method is easy and quick and gives a sturdy door. The corners are cut at a forty-five degree angle with a miter saw and nailed

Ground dwelling birds such as button quail (left) and silver pheasants (facing page) can be interesting and colorful additions to an aviary.

together at the corners with corrugated nails. The small inside doors were made with one by two material, the large outside flight cage doors by one by fours. On these a corner plate with four screws was used at each inside corner.

"By spring the inside was complete and painted water lily green and the inside cage walls covered with a whitewash containing a mite-killer. I have used this for years in my chicken house with good success.

"I was now busy with other things until fall when Charlie, my father-in-law, came for his annual visit. Preparations were made for building the outside flights. The flights were three feet wide and eleven feet eight inches long allowing for the use of three foot wide wire and with a two and a half foot door. A trench for a concrete footing was dug and the footing poured and leveled. In order to save making forms I decided to use cement blocks. As the ground slopes away from the building on the north, the wall is three blocks high and only

one on the south. The spaces in the blocks were filled with cement and some eye bolts embedded about five feet in both directions from the corners. To these eye bolts wires were run to the upper corners for braces. A turnbuckle was used on each wire for tightening the wires.

"It is probably not necessary to go into much detail in construction of the flights. Two by fours were used on edge for the sills on the foundation and for the partitions and also for the top. The uprights were two by twos except for two by fours on which the doors were hinged. Mass production principles were used in sawing. All pieces to be of the same length were cut by placing the long boards side by side on saw horses and cutting through them all at once with the power saw. Three lengths of two by twos were put crosswise of the top of the flights for added strength and to help prevent sagging of the wire. So that the top would be flush, notches were cut in the two by fours into which the two by twos

151

fit. These were cut by placing all these two by fours side by side on edge, marking by laying a two by two across them, then with the power saw set at the proper depth sawing along the marks. The notches were then cut out with a chisel.

"As stated, the flights are three feet wide, as are the inside cages except one. Because of the corner taken up by the sink, one is six feet wide, and in this I made a small pool using a wash tub for the inner form. In this I hope to have a pair of ornamental ducks.

"The space between the ground level and the top of the foundation was filled with large rocks and the surface leveled with crushed rock as used for highways. I thought this would provide drainage and better sanitation, be more practical than trying to maintain grass, and cheaper than concrete.

"The wire on the south is of one-third inch mesh as on the cages, while on the north one inch hexagonal chicken wire was used, except on the two prospective parrot pens which are of two by four inch welded wire.

"There is a perch at either end, the one being under the eaves. Small doors with a landing board lead from the inside to the flight and are closed when necessary. On the south where there are upper and lower cages, there are two rows of doors, and I hope the lower floor occupants do not try to live upstairs.

"I now have parrakeets, lovebirds, cockatiels, various finches, a toucan, a myna, and a squirrel, which will have to go out as I get more birds. I recently moved in some pheasants, as the drenching rains turned their pens into wading pools. In outside pens I have five varieties of pheasants: Golden, Amherst, Silver, Reeves and Black-throated Golden. At large are Indian blue peafowl and pearl guineas.

"I hope to add more finches, rice birds, weavers, large and small parrots, doves, quail, magpies, and other birds as the desire may develop.

"The completed bird house presents a very neat appearance in its natural setting on a little knoll surrounded by fir and pine trees. Since I am no architect, I carried the plans in my head to the dismay of my helpers, my wife, her father, and our three boys and a girl, all of whom took part. Many details were worked out as we went along. Also, not being a carpenter, some little crudities could be found and some corners not exactly plumb. Perhaps because of our inexperience, we derived more pleasure from our work and more pride in our achievement. Our birds have created a great deal of interest in this area, which is quite isolated from any large cities where one can see bird collections. Now that we have plenty of room I tell visitors to come again as we will have something new next time."

The prospective builder of an outdoor birdroom should first consider three essentials when designing his structure: good lighting, good ventilation, and adequate protection from extremes of heat and cold.

A Michigan fancier converted a 20 by 20 stucco garage into an aviary. A vestibule was built to shed snow, etc., and to provide an entrance trap in the event birds are loose in the aviary. Only budgerigars are raised.

Along the north wall are 4 flights, each 8 feet long and so arranged that they may be subdivided into 4 sections. Lower flights are 30 inches high, top flights 38 inches high. To prevent the birds from flying into the glass of the windows at the back of the top flights, plastic has been installed. This still permits the light to enter.

Along the east wall are 20 breeding cages constructed as cabinets in units of two. Overall size, 39 inches high, 30 inches wide, 16 inches deep. This may be made into two cages by inserting a center divider, pan and screen. Then each cage is approximately 19 inches high. Outside of breeding season, the divider is removed and the space is used as a small flight.

Transom type windows minimize drafts when open. Cages

This aviary, constructed around a large eucalyptus tree, was constructed to provide a home for cockatiels.

This aviary, now under repair, was used to colony-breed Bourke's parakeets. The structure was 7′ high, 7′ wide and 40′ long.

are set on a base containing drawers providing ample storage space for miscellaneous equipment. A compact seed bin provides handy storage for 800 pounds of seed, 600 pounds of gravel, and 200 pounds of oats.

The ceiling is 10 feet high, giving ample cubic footage for good ventilation. There are 4 fluorescent lights and two 48 inch germicidal units, including one in the seed bin.

A drop leaf table, on casters, with drawers for dishes and utensils, is used for feeding, and whenever bench space is needed.

To permit a more diversified seed diet without cluttering the bottom of the cage, dishes are on doors which swing out, two on each side. This also simplifies the feeding operation.

Wire fronts are held in place by three-fourths inch aluminum square rod, which is held in place by screws at the ends. Wire front has a door large enough to admit the nest box. The door matches the rest of the front and is very simple in construction. Aluminum rods on sides and back hold the bottoms and pans.

Each cage is equipped with a card holder (2 x 5) for nest record. A white card is used for the first nest, a salmon card for the second nest. A small hook on the back wall of the plywood cage holds a two hole feeder which is used only when the pair is feeding young. The only dish which is ever placed on the floor is one used for soaked seeds when chicks are being fed.

In a large city backyard aviary, temperature is controlled at 65 degrees summer and winter. One of its greatest features is the fresh running water which flows continuously through breeding boxes and insures plenty of fresh and cool water at all times.

Seed and grit are placed in an automatic hopper which holds about one pound of seed. Hulls fall to the bottom and are easily removed. Nest boxes are numbered, and a card on each lists all vital statistics regarding the breeding pair.

The outdoor flight is 18 feet long, eight feet deep and eight and one-half feet high. It is connected to the interior by three large hinged windows which are opened when weather permits. On either side of each of these windows is a small opening which is open at all times, giving the birds access to the outdoor flight at all times. Some time after it was built, the flights were glassed in, but at no time is this area heated. One flight is for females, the center one for males, and the other for young birds.

From Ohio, where the range in temperature is great, we have a description of an aviary in which the outside flight is 12 by 16 feet. There is a large bush in which this fancier hopes his robins will nest.

The inside flight is 12 by 18 feet and is heated by baseboard radiant heating. It contains a fish pond, fountain, and tropical plants. While some shade is provided by nearby trees, on very hot days the birds often stay inside.

A New York couple reports success in breeding two pairs of budgies in a large flight cage in their bedroom, even though the room doubled as a playroom for their young sons. Their new hobby so fascinated them that they are now expanding their bird raising project to a complete outdoor aviary.

A very large European aviary houses five thousand birds and is situated in Holland. Its dimensions are: 82 yards long, 18 feet wide, and 14 feet high. Down the middle of this imposing structure runs a beech hedge, forty years old. Forty odd species of birds are represented among thousands of occupants.